Jagdgeschwader 7 'Nowotny'

Jagdgeschwader 7 'Nowotny'

Robert Forsyth

Series editor Tony Holmes

Front Cover

On 22 March 1945, a formation of 27 Me 262s from the *Geschwader Stabsschwarm* and III./JG 7, led by the commander of JG 7, Knight's Cross holder Major Theodor Weissenberger, attacked B-17Gs of the 483rd Bomb Group's 817th Bomb Squadron between Leipzig and their target of the day, the synthetic fuel plant at Ruhland, north of Dresden. The Flying Fortresses of the USAAF's Fifteenth Air Force had flown from their bases in Italy on a deep penetration raid, and they were on the approach to their bomb run at a height of 6000 metres over central Germany when the Me 262s struck.

Scrambled from Parchim to intercept, Major Weissenberger was flying Me 262A-1a 'Green 4', with its distinctive *Kommodore* markings, when he shot down one of the 483rd's B-17s. Mark Postlethwaite's specially commissioned cover artwork depicts the moment of Weissenberger's kill, his jet force having made its approach in line abreast from above and to the rear of the American formation, while Me 262A-1a 'Yellow 7' of Oberfeldwebel Heinz Arnold from 11./JG 7 fires off its underwing battery of 55 mm R4M missiles to bring down a second bomber.

Altogether, JG 7 would claim 12 B-17s destroyed during this interception. The Fifteenth Air Force subsequently acknowledged the loss of 11 Flying Fortresses (six from the 483rd BG and five from the 2nd BG) to enemy fighters and one to flak (*Cover artwork by Mark Postlethwaite*)

DEDICATION

To Eddie and Richard – a 'snippet'(!) in recognition of your inspiration and friendship over the past 18 years

First published in Great Britain in 2008 by Osprey Publishing
Midland House, West Way, Botley, Oxford, OX2 0PH
443 Park Avenue South, New York, NY, 10016, USA
E-mail; info@ospreypublishing.com

ISBN 13; 978 1 84603 320 9

Edited by Tony Holmes
Page design by Mark Holt
Cover Artwork by Mark Postlethwaite
Aircraft Profiles by Jim Laurier
Originated by PDQ Digital Media Solutions
Printed and bound in China through Bookbuilders
Index by Alan Thatcher

Printed and bound in China through Book Builders

08 09 10 11 12   10 9 8 7 6 5 4 3 2 1

ACKNOWLEDGEMENTS

I would like to acknowledge the kind contributions of Nick Beale, Walter J Boyne, Eddie Creek, Peter Petrick, J Richard Smith and Hans-Heiri Stapfer during the preparation of this volume. I would also like to acknowledge Manfred Boehme's study into the history of JG 7, as his book is essential reading for anyone wanting to enquire further into the fascinating history of this unit (see Bibliography).

EDITOR'S NOTE

To make this best-selling series as authoritative as possible, the Editor would be interested in hearing from any individual who may have relevant photographs, documentation or first-hand experiences relating to the world's elite pilots, and their aircraft, of the various theatres of war. Any material used will be credited to its original source. Please write to Tony Holmes via e-mail at: tony.holmes@zen.co.uk

CONTENTS

EVOLUTION

In many respects, the partnership between Walter Nowotny and Karl Schnörrer typified the lives of Luftwaffe fighter pilots during the middle years of World War 2. One became a famous *Experte*, the other would earn a reputation as a first rate wingman. Yet, the former would be killed flying what – at the time – was the world's most technologically advanced fighter aircraft, while the latter would fly the same type of machine – despite severe injuries – to the end of the war and survive. That aircraft was the Messerschmitt Me 262.

Nowotny, Austrian by birth, had entered the Luftwaffe in October 1939, and in 1941 he had joined JG 54, quickly being posted to the Eastern Front. The young, still novice, pilot claimed his first aerial victories over Ösel Island in July, when he shot down two Russian I-153 biplanes, but was himself shot down in the same engagement and subsequently spent three days and nights at sea in a rubber dinghy. However, he went on to shoot down five Russian fighters on 20 July, and on 11 August he destroyed two more. Although sustaining hits to his Bf 109G-2, Nowotny managed to nurse his badly damaged aircraft back to base and crash-land, although suffering injuries in the process.

In recognition of a seemingly meteoric subsequent service record, Leutnant Nowotny was awarded the Knight's Cross on 4 September for his accumulated 56 victories and was appointed *Staffelkapitän* of 1./JG 54 of the now famous *Grünherz Geschwader* in late October 1942 (see *Osprey Aviation Elite Units 6 - Jagdgeschwader 54 'Grünherz'* for further details). By 15 June the following year, he had registered his 100th victory, and on 10 August 1943, he was appointed *Gruppenkommandeur* of I./JG 54. On 1 September 1943, Nowotny shot down ten enemy aircraft – five in the space of 12 minutes in the morning, with a further five within nine minutes around midday. The following day he downed six more!

The Oakleaves to the Knight's Cross followed on 4 September when Nowotny's score stood at 189 victories, and within four days he had shot down his 200th kill. The then Hauptmann Nowotny received the coveted Swords in September for 218 victories, and went on to achieve 250 kills – a score which, at the time, made him the world's ranking fighter ace. On 19 October he became the eighth recipient of the Diamonds, which was then the highest award for operational service that could be presented to a Luftwaffe pilot.

At that point, Adolf Hitler decided to withdraw Nowotny from the risks associated with combat on the Eastern Front and use him at home as a propaganda icon – where, in many ways, he could be just as valuable. He left for France in early February 1944, having amassed a score totalling 255 victories.

Karl Schnörrer, who was a native of Nürnberg, also served with I./JG 54, and claimed his first victory over the Eastern Front in December 1941. In late 1942, Nowotny selected Feldwebel Schnörrer to fly as his *Kaczmarek* (wingman), and the two fighter pilots subsequently became close friends.

An ace and his wingman. Walter Nowotny (left), seen here as *Kommandeur* of I./JG 54, listens to Karl Schnörrer describe an aerial encounter over Russia in 1943 shortly after returning from another mission. Nowotny was awarded the Diamonds to the Knights' Cross in October 1943 – the eighth such recipient – at which point he left the Eastern Front on the express orders of Hitler. The following month, after being injured when baling out of his Fw 190 too low to the ground, Schnörrer also left Russia. In the autumn of 1944 Nowotny was made commander of a new Me 262-equipped fighter unit that bore his name, and the two pilots were duly reunited when Schnörrer was posted to the *Kommando*

Despite a reputation for being a hard man on his aircraft following three landing accidents whilst at the controls of Bf 109s, Schnörrer became an invaluable and trusted partner to Nowotny during the latter's stellar rise as a fighter ace. It is perhaps a measure of his priorities, that Schnörrer, who had earned himself the slightly unjust nickname of *'Quax'* after an accident-prone cartoon character, had scored 20 victories by 18 August 1943, against his flight leader's score of 151. However, on 12 November 1943, both pilots embarked on their last mission on the Eastern Front when they took part in extensive air operations over the Nevel area.

Engaging a formation of Soviet Il-2 *Shturmoviks*, Nowotny shot one down for his 255th victory and Schnörrer destroyed another one when it attempted to attack Nowotny's aircraft. This would be Schnörrer's 35th victory, but it would come at a cost, as he recalled;

'I had flown operations in Russia in the Bf 109 and Fw 190. On 12 November 1943, I was shot down and badly injured after I had got my 35th Russian aircraft. I had baled out too low for my parachute to open and came down into some trees. I had concussion, my ribs were broken, both my knees were broken and my arms were broken. German infantry rescued me from no-man's land.

'Generaloberst *Ritter* von Greim, the commander of *Luftflotte* 6, ordered that I should be flown back to Germany in his personal He 111 to receive the best treatment that was possible. Nowotny escorted me back.'

In the meantime, Nowotny had been ordered to take command of a fighter training unit, JG 101, in southern France – a relatively safe role which he assumed in February 1944. After some quiet months in his relatively dull French 'backwater' at Pau, Nowotny made an excited visit to his old friend, 'Quax', who was still recovering from his injuries. 'Once every three weeks or so Nowotny would visit me in hospital and bring me food, drink and cigarettes', Schnörrer recalled. 'On one such visit he said to me, "Quax, we're going to get a very new aircraft – a jet aircraft". That was in the summer of 1944, and I made my first flight in an Me 262 that year, with my legs still in plaster'.

Professor Willy Messerschmitt's state-of-the-art fighter had first taken to the air using pure jet power on 18 July 1942 when company test pilot Fritz Wendel made a trouble-free flight from Leipheim. Following a delayed gestation, largely attributable to setbacks and problems with engine development and supply from BMW and Junkers, Wendel was able to report generally smooth handling during the maiden test-flight, during which he achieved an unprecedented airspeed of 720 km/h. Despite misgivings, Wendel also recorded that the Junkers T1 engines had 'worked well'.

Germany now possessed the technology it needed to respond to the ever-growing threat of Allied air power in the West.

Ominous events overshadowed the Me 262's development programme when, in mid-1944, a number of early series aircraft suffered mishaps. Here, Me 262 S3 Wk-Nr. 130008 VI+AH is seen having crash-landed at Lechfeld on 16 June. Both turbojet engines were ripped off as a result of the crash and the nose, wings and undercarriage were also damaged

From then on, until mid-1944, development on the Me 262 forged ahead using a series of prototypes to test all aspects of the aircraft. There were highs and lows. *Dipl.-Ing.* Heinrich Beauvais crashed the Me 262 V3 in August 1942 after three abortive attempts to take off. On 18 April 1943, Oberfeldwebel Wilhelm Ostertag was killed when one of the Jumo 004 turbojets on the Me 262 V2 flamed out, throwing the jet into a steep dive from which it never recovered. Later, in May 1944, Unteroffizier Kurt Flachs was killed when the Me 262 V7 crashed on its 31st flight.

The first series production aircraft were also plagued by problems too, suffering from burst tyres, electrical and mechanical maladies and persistent engine flame-outs. In June 1944 alone, the S7 crashed on the 1st following an engine fire, the Me 262 S1 suffered a damaged starboard wing on the 11th, while the fuselage nose, wings and both engines of the S3 were damaged in a crash landing at Lechfeld on the 16th.

Nevertheless, the Luftwaffe had been advocating the potential benefits of the Me 262 for some time. Persuaded by Messerschmitt, as early as 17 April 1943, Hauptmann Wolfgang Späte (a 72-victory Knight's Cross holder and former *Staffelkapitän* of 5./JG 54) flew the Me 262 V2 – the first Luftwaffe pilot to do so. Two days later he reported to the *General der Jagdflieger*, Generalmajor Adolf Galland;

'Flight characteristics are such that an experienced fighter pilot would be able to handle the aircraft. In particular, the increase in air speed when compared to the fastest conventional fighter deserves attention. This is not expected to decrease markedly when armament and radio equipment have been fitted.

'Characteristically, jet engines will not only maintain this speed at altitude, but increase it. The climbing speed of the Me 262 surpasses that of the Bf 109G by five to six metres per second at a much better speed. The superior horizontal and climbing speeds will enable the aircraft to operate successfully against numerically superior enemy fighters. The extremely heavy armament (six 30 mm guns) permits attacks on bombers at high approach speeds with destructive results, despite the short time the aircraft is in the firing position.'

On 17 April 1943, Me 262 V2 Wk-Nr. 262 000 0002 PC+UB, distinctive here through the absence of the aircraft's familiar nosewheel, was assessed in flight by Major Wolfgang Späte, a 72-victory Knight's Cross holder and former *Staffelkapitän* of 5./JG 54. Späte subsequently reported that, in his view, with its combination of high performance and heavy armament, the jet fighter would be able to prove efficient against both enemy fighters and bombers. However, the very next day, the same machine nose-dived and crashed, killing test pilot Oberfeldwebel Wilhelm Ostertag, following an engine flame-out

Firepower – the 'sharp end' of an Me 262A-1a, showing the standard installation of four MK 108 30 mm cannon in the nose. The MK 108 was manufactured by Rheinmetall-Borsig, and it proved to be a deadly weapon during close-range combat with heavy bombers. Although a powerful weapon, the MK 108's cheapness and ease of manufacture made it prone to jamming and other forms of malfunction

Leutnant Günther Wegmann served as adjutant to the commanders of both *Erprobungskommando* 262 and *Kommando Nowotny*. He later led 11./JG 7, but was severely wounded on 18 March 1945 when his Me 262 was hit by defensive fire from a B-17 over Glöwen. Wegmann baled out but eventually suffered the amputation of one of his legs following the incident

This was music to Galland's ears. On 22 May 1943, he flew the Me 262 V4 himself at Lechfeld (after an attempt to start the engines of the V3 resulted in a fire) and made his famous report to *Reichsmarschall* Göring in which he enthused 'It felt as if angels were pushing!' Galland became a firm advocate for the further development of the jet, and wrote to his superiors that all measures should be taken to ensure swift and large-scale production of the aircraft. In a report to Generalluftzeugmeister Erhard Milch he wrote, 'The aircraft represents a great step forward and could be our greatest chance. It could guarantee us an unimaginable lead over the enemy if he adheres to the piston engine'.

The Me 262 eventually emerged as a twin-engined jet fighter powered by two Jumo 004 turbojet units. At the heart of each engine was an eight-stage axial compressor with single-stage turbines producing 8.8 kN of thrust at 8700 rpm. In the standard Me 262A-1a fighter/interceptor configuration, it was to be armed with four formidable MK 108 30 mm cannon mounted in the nose.

The first assessment of the aircraft in operational conditions was made by *Erprobungskommando* 262, which had been commanded since August 1944 by Hauptmann Horst Geyer. This small test unit consisted of three *Einsatzkommandos* based at Lechfeld, Rechlin-Lärz and Erfurt-Bindersleben, and comprised a number of pilots of varying experience drawn from numerous *Jagd-* and *Zerstörergeschwader*.

In September, Galland instigated some structural changes to the unit, assigning the staff echelon of the *Kommando* as the nucleus of a new III. *Gruppe, Erganzungsjagdgeschwader* 2 at Lechfeld intended to oversee all future jet fighter training, while the component *Einsatzkommandos* were moved north to the concrete runways at Hesepe and Achmer. The latter bases provided a suitable environment from which to embark on regular missions in the defence of the Reich, using the undoubted technological superiority of the new Messerschmitt to intercept Allied heavy bombers and their piston-engined escort fighters.

On paper, this organisation appeared acceptable enough, but the reality was very different. Despite a strength of some 30 Me 262A-1as, most of the *Kommandos'* pilots remained largely untrained on the jet fighter, and their new bases lay directly in the approach paths of those USAAF bombers, and their escorts, which were beginning to appear in ever greater numbers in German airspace.

It was at this time that Galland plucked Walter Nowotny from France in order to lead the newly formed *Kommando Nowotny*, which had been formed from the Achmer and Hesepe units. Nowotny's *Kommando* was established with a *Stab* of four aircraft, together with three *Staffeln*, each with a nominal strength of 16 Me 262s. As an adjutant, Nowotny was assigned Oberleutnant Günther Wegmann, who had served as adjutant to Geyer, with Hauptmann Streicher as Technical Officer.

The 1. *Staffel* was led by Oberleutnant Paul Bley, while commanding 2. *Staffel* was Oberleutnant Alfred Teumer, with Hauptmann Georg-Peter Eder leading 3. *Staffel*. A former *Gruppenkommandeur* of II./JG 1, Eder had been awarded the Knight's Cross while serving as *Kapitän* of 6./JG 26. Briefly appointed *Kommandeur* of II./JG 26 in September 1944, he was transferred to *Erprobungskommando* 262 the same month. Eder had 54 victories to his name.

There followed a brief period of familiarisation during which Nowotny and his old friend from the Eastern Front, 'Quax' Schnörrer, flew the Me 262 for the first time. Fortunately for Schnörrer, the plaster on his legs had come off, and before flying the jet he had piloted the Bf 110 at Kaufbeuren in order to familiarise himself with asymmetric flying. He remembered;

'There was a wonderful feeling of effortless speed and power. But each aircraft flew with only 2500 litres of J2 fuel. After about 12.5 hours, the turbine units had to be changed. We flew for about 40-60 minutes, then had to land. We had to be very careful with the throttles, and had to advance them very, very slowly or there was a risk of fire.

'The engines were started using a Riedel starter unit. The turbines were run up to 1800 rpm and then C3 fuel was used to light up the Jumo. The throttle was advanced very, very slowly until at 3000 rpm you could switch to J2 fuel. Again, one had to advance the throttles very slowly to 6000 rpm, and as one increased to 8000 rpm, the throttles could be used a little faster. Both Nowotny and Günther Wegmann suffered turbine fires because they advanced the throttles too rapidly.

'As soon as we reached 8400 rpm, it was off with the brakes and off we went. Because they used so much fuel, the Me 262s were usually started up in position to begin a take-off run. As soon as you were off the ground, you had to retract the undercarriage. The other pilots told me, "It isn't difficult, but make sure you do everything in the climb and not in the descent. If you let the aircraft get into a dive and the speed rises over 1000 km/h, you won't get out". At high altitude, one had to be careful not to throttle back too far or the motor would flame out.'

Problems plagued *Kommando Nowotny* from the start. Despite a somewhat crude training programme, it was found that only 15 pilots – those possessing any experience at all on the Me 262 – were capable of flying the type. By late September, however, the *Kommando* had some 30 Me 262s. The following month saw the first tentative operations, but in

Knight's Cross holder Hauptmann Georg-Peter Eder served as *Gruppenkommandeur* of II./JG 1 and II./JG 26 before flying the Me 262 with *Erprobungskommando 262* and *Kommando Nowotny*. He later served with III./JG 7, but suffered severe injuries when he struck his aircraft while baling out after having engaged heavy bombers near Bremen on 17 February 1945

Me 262A-1as of *Kommando Nowotny* are refuelled whilst parked on the concrete perimeter track at Achmer in the autumn of 1944 – a tempting target for marauding USAAF P-47s or P-51s

Taken a little later than the photograph on page 11, these *Kommando Nowotny* aircraft have now been refuelled and will soon be taken out to the runway at Achmer by the semi-tracked Kettenkrad tow tractor seen hooked up to 'White 5', closest to the camera. The Kettenkrads were extensively used by Me 262 units in an effort to save precious aviation fuel

'White 5' is hauled away by a Kettenkrad, although it may be heading for maintenance rather than a mission judging by the engine panels resting on the uppersurface of the jet's left wing. Note the uniform tail markings of all the Me 262A-1as seen in this series of photographs, as well as the yellow fuselage bands and large tactical numerals on their noses – all markings associated with *Kommando Nowotny*. 'White 19' has an electric starter cart parked alongside it

the first half of October, no fewer than ten jets were either destroyed or damaged due to take-off or landing accidents. Nowotny's pilots, most of them drawn from conventional single-engined fighter units, lacking sufficient training in instrument flying and with only two or three dedicated training flights, found the Me 262 with its effortless speed, short endurance and rapid descent difficult to handle.

On its second day of operations, the unit suffered the loss of Oberleutnant Teumer (a veteran of 300+ missions with JG 54, Teumer had claimed 76 kills and been awarded the Knight's Cross in August 1944) when an engine flamed out and he crashed and burned while landing at Hesepe. That same day, the man who would replace Teumer as leader of 2./*Kommando Nowotny*, Leutnant Franz Schall, had a lucky escape when his jet crashed on landing at Waggum following a technical fault. It was a stark warning to others that the Me 262 could not be taken for granted.

The *Kommando* attempted to fly its first operational sortie 'in force' on 7 October against one of the largest American daylight bombing raids so far mounted, aimed at oil targets at Pölitz, Ruhland, Merseburg and Lutzkendorf. Taking off from Hesepe, Leutnant Schall and Feldwebel Heinz Lennartz, who had joined the embryonic *Ekdo 262* from 5./JG 11, each managed to claim a B-24 shot down, thus bringing home the *Kommando's* first victories. However, it would be different for those aircraft operating from Achmer.

As Oberleutnant Bley, Leutnant Gerhard Kobert and Oberfähnrich Heinz Russel prepared to take-off, a P-51D from the 361st FG, piloted by ace 1Lt Urban L Drew, swooped down from 5000 metres to open fire on the Me 262s lining up for take off. Russel's aircraft collapsed under the American's machine gun fire, Kobert's aircraft blew up and Bley's machine crashed, but he was able to bale out.

Isolated victories against Mustangs on 10 and 12 October did little to counter the scything opinions of Fritz Wendel, who visited *Kommando Nowotny* as part of a Messerschmittt technical field team;

'*Kommando Nowotny* has been in action since 3 October 1944. Up until 24 October, sorties had been flown on a total of three days. The Inspector of the Day Fighters, Oberst Trautloft, was at the base during the first days, and had made great personal efforts to ensure the success of the first fighter sorties with the Me 262. He saw to it that several successful fighter pilots were taken from other units to form the core of this unit. The commander, Major Nowotny is a successful Eastern Front pilot, but is unfamiliar with the present situation in the West and, at 23, is not the superior leader personality necessary to guarantee the success of this vital operation.'

Wendel went on to demolish the unit's operational and tactical methods and lack of a coherent objective, pointing out contradictory opinions within its personnel. He concluded by stating that, 'Instruction on the aircraft type is particularly bad with *Kommando Nowotny*. The importance given to the technical side may be illustrated by the fact that the *Gruppe* Technical Officer at Achmer, Hauptmann Streicher, is not a technician. The *Staffel* Technical Officer at Hesepe, 19-year-old Oberfähnrich Russel, is also a complete layman, who has himself recently destroyed two aircraft as a result of carelessness and inadequate training'.

As if this was not harmful enough to Galland's efforts to champion the Me 262 as the fighter that would save Germany, circumstances were now playing into the hands of those who saw a very different role for the jet – that of a high-speed bomber. Already, comparatively more favourable results were being achieved by KG 51, which had recently commenced flying operations in the Rhine area with the jet in the bombing role.

In May 1944, Adolf Hitler had declared his irritation that the Me 262 had not been adapted to carry bombs with which to operate as a high-speed bomber against any Allied seaborne invasion of Europe. Even in his April 1943 report, Wolfgang Späte had observed 'as a fighter-bomber, and carrying bombs, the aircraft would still be faster than any enemy fighter'.

Leutnant Franz Schall, leader of 2./*Kommando Nowotny* (left) stands in front of an Me 262 from the unit, probably at Achmer, in the autumn of 1944. Later appointed *Staffelkapitän* of 10./JG 7, he would ultimately see more air combat in the Me 262 than most jet pilots

Feldwebel Heinz Lennartz transferred to flying the Me 262 with *Erprobungskommando* 262 and *Kommando Nowotny* from JG 11. Among the first of the Me 262 pilots to claim an enemy bomber shot down, he would survive the war as a jet 'veteran' flying with III./JG 7

In October 1944, Messerschmitt test pilot Fritz Wendel wrote an acerbic report on the accomplishments – or perhaps the lack of them – of *Kommando Nowotny*. He believed that the unit's training methods were 'particularly bad'

Despite criticism from Fritz Wendel, *Kommando Nowotny* pressed on with operations until early November 1944. To the left of this photograph, pilots hold a pre-flight briefing, while to the right, mechanics check the Jumo 004 turbojets. It would all come to an end, on 7 November, however, when Major Walter Nowotny was shot down by P-51s and killed returning from a sortie against USAAF heavy bombers

Kommando Nowotny struggled on into November. Oberfähnrich Willi Banzhaff of 3.*Staffel* was forced to bale out following an encounter with P-51s over Holland on the 1st, but 24 hours later there was some cheer when a P-51 and a P-47 were downed by Feldwebel Erich Büttner, with a a second Thunderbolt falling to Oberfeldwebel Helmut Baudach. However, these events were tempered by the loss of Unteroffizier Alois Zollner, who was killed when his Me 262 crashed on take-off from Achmer. Three more jets were lost on 4 November in a single action with Mustangs.

Two days later, four Me 262s from the *Kommando* were damaged, three of them in emergency landings apparently as a result of fuel shortages. A solitary success for the unit that same day came when Leutnant Franz Schall destroyed a P-47.

Worse was to come when Galland, already concerned at the increasing losses being suffered by his only jet fighter unit, arrived at Achmer on 7 November for an inspection. The next day, as the USAAF bombed the Nordhorn Canal and the marshalling yards at Rheine, the *Kommando* was able to despatch just four jets in two missions against the bombers. There was an inauspicious beginning when Nowotny found that he was unable to start his aircraft for the first mission in the morning, while another machine suffered a burst tyre.

In the second mission, that afternoon, Nowotny finally took off to engage the enemy at the controls of 'White 8'. During his subsequent encounter, the ace shot down a four-engined bomber and a P-51, but as he returned home, he was apparently intercepted by another USAAF Mustang – believed to have been from either the 20th, 357th or 364th FGs. A short while later, Nowotny's crackling voice was heard over the radio. 'We stepped into the open', Galland later wrote. 'Visibility was not good – six-tenths cloud. Seconds later an Me 262 appeared out of the cloud and dived vertically into the ground. There was black smoke and an explosion'. Nowotny's last words, though garbled, indicated that his aircraft was hit and on fire, and seconds later he crashed to his death.

FORMATION

The death of Walter Nowotny effectively marked the end of the *Kommando* that bore his name, but the honour title – together with the further deployment of the aircraft that his unit had flown – would re-emerge as the name adopted by a much larger, more structured unit over the forthcoming weeks.

In August 1944, following a proposal from the office of the *General der Jagdflieger*, the OKL had authorised the establishiment of a new *Jagdgeschwader* (to be known as JG 7) consisting of two Fw 190-equipped *Gruppen* based at Königsberg. The cadre of personnel for this new *Geschwader* was to be drawn from the idling bomber unit KG 1 'Hindenburg', for which there had been vague plans for conversion onto the Bf 109 as part of IX. *Fliegerkorps.* The new scheme was that the *Stab* II./KG 1 would form the new *Stab* I./JG 7 under the command of Hauptmann Gerhard Baeker, with 1., 2., 3. and 4./JG 7 being formed from 5., 6., 7. and 8./KG 1 respectively.

All the units remained at Königsberg with the exception of 2./JG 7, which was detached to Zieghenhain, in Czechoslovakia, although an 'advanced detachment' of I./JG 7 was reported at Pomssen on 9 November. A second *Gruppe*, II./JG 7, was planned using *Stab* III./KG 1 as its *Stab* and 9./KG 1 as 5./JG 7, but with 6., 7. and 8./JG 7 formed as brand new units.

However, the demand for replacement aircraft by the already over-stretched existing fighter *Geschwader* operating in the defence of the Reich, combined with a worsening shortage of pilots, meant that the proposal had to be shelved. It was reinstated by the OKL in October, and this time JG 7 was to be re-equipped with Bf 109G-14s and its II. *Gruppe* based at Zieghenhain. But once again the pressing realities of the air war over the Reich meant that this proposal could not actually be carried out.

Then, over the course of a four-day armaments conference between 1-4 November, Adolf Hitler finally gave his permission for the Me 262 to be built as a fighter, but under the strict proviso that the aircraft could quickly be made capable of carrying at least one 250-kg bomb if neccesary. This gave Galland the opportunity to move ahead with the establishment of a new jet-equipped fighter unit that would be assigned the redundant designation *Jagdgeschwader 7*. A few days later on 12 November, matters were confirmed when OKL issued official orders that JG 7 was not to be equipped with piston-engined aircraft.

Galland selected Oberst Johannes Steinhoff as *Kommodore* of the new *Geschwader.* Thirty-two-year-old 'Macki' Steinhoff was an accomplished, veteran, fighter pilot. A graduate in philology from the University of Jena in 1934, he subsequently attended both naval and Luftwaffe training schools. Transferring to the Luftwaffe from the Kriegsmarine in 1936, Steinhoff embodied the ideal blend of social values and military discipline, and by 1938 he had been given his first command as *Staffelkapitän* of 10(N)./JG 26. This was a hastily organised nightfighter unit equipped with the Bf 109C which, in December 1939 – having converted back to

the day fighter role – engaged in the well-publicised attack on RAF Wellingtons despatched to bomb warships at Wilhelmshaven. Steinhoff shot down one bomber in what became one of the earliest organised interceptions of a daylight bomber raid.

Steinhoff led 4./JG 52 during the fighting over the English Channel in 1940. His style of command was known to be fair-minded and professional. Steinhoff was awarded the Knight's Cross on 30 August 1941 and appointed *Kommandeur* of II./JG 52 on 28 February 1942. By 31 August 1942, Steinhoff had chalked up 100 aerial kills, and he received the Oakleaves two days later. On 24 March he was transferred from the Eastern Front to Tunisia, where he assumed command of JG 77. Steinhoff subsequently led the unit in North Africa and then through the maelstrom of air combat over Sicily and Italy, engaging American heavy bombers and their escorts and steadily adding kills to his personal score. In late July 1944 he was awarded the Swords to his Knight's Cross to recognise his 167th aerial victory.

From August 1944, however, the component *Gruppen* of JG 77 were progressively transferred back to the Reich, and by October they were clustered on bases around Berlin. In November, Steinhoff was ordered to attend a conference organised by *Reichsmarschall* Göring at the *Luftskriegsakademie* Gatow that was intended to 'restore the Luftwaffe to full striking power in the shortest possible time'. In what became known as the *'Aeropag'*, a carefully selected gathering of some 40 senior officers from the fighter, bomber, reconnaissance and ground-attack arms met in an attempt to resolve divisions and differences of opinions that existed within their ranks.

The deterioration in the relationship between Adolf Galland as *General der Jagdflieger* and a number of forceful officers on his staff was to prove instrumental in exacerbating the growing sense of spiritlessness that seeped through certain senior echelons of the *Jagdwaffe* in late 1944 in the face of a worsening air war against the Allies. Steinhoff, who had long been a great supporter of Galland, was appalled by the untenable position into which his commanding general had been placed. He duly embarked upon machinations with a handful of other disgruntled fighter commanders and Knight's Cross holders, including Oberst Günther Lützow, Oberst Gustav Rödel, Oberst Günther von Maltzahn and Oberst Hannes Traut-loft that were designed to depose Göring, who they saw as the prinicipal architect of the downfall of the *Jagdwaffe*.

But before such plots could get underway, Galland assigned Steinhoff as commander of the new JG 7. For Steinhoff, it was an unexpected appointment. He recorded in his memoirs, as the assembled officers sat around the conference table several hours in to the so-called '*Aeropag*', 'Galland passed me a note. It read, "Under pressure from the *Führer*, the *Reichsmarschall* has given permission for the first jet-fighter group to be set up. Do you want to command it?" My first reaction was to wonder why he bothered to ask. Did he think I was likely to refuse an offer like that? I scribbled two words on the note and passed it back – "Many thanks!"'

On 19 November, what remained of *Kommando Nowotny* at Lechfeld was redesignated III./JG 7 and transferred to Brandenburg-Briest, where it joined the *Geschwaderstab*. Here, the *Stab* and signals section of *Kommando Nowotny* became the *Stab* and signals section of the new III. *Gruppe*, while 1., 2. and 3./*Kommando Nowotny* became 9., 10. and 11./JG 7, respectively, all of which would function under the command of 1. *Jagdkorps* and be supplied by *Luftgau* III. The planned establishment of 4./*Kommando Nowotny* was cancelled.

The *Gruppe* was augmented by flying, ground and technical personnel from the recently disbanded KG 1 '*Hindenburg*', whose honour title the new *Geschwader* would adopt for a brief period. Simultaneously, the originally planned I./JG 7, to be formed from II./KG 1, was slated to be redesignated as II./JG 7 on 24 November, with 1., 2., 3. and 4./JG 7 forming a new 5., 6., 7. and 8./JG 7. I./JG 7 was reformed the following day at Königsberg from II./JG 3, with 5./JG 3 becoming 1./JG 7, 7./JG 3 becoming 2./JG 7 and 8./JG 3 becoming 3./JG 7.

The planned II./JG 7, to be formed from elements of III./KG 1, was redesignated on 24 November as a new IV./JG 301, with 5., 6., 7. and 8./JG 7 becoming 13., 14., 15. and 16./JG 301, respectively. This new *Jagdgruppe* was also to take over the '*Hindenburg*' title from JG 7.

The new *Geschwader* would fall under the tactical control of Oberst Heinrich Wittmer's 1. *Jagddivision* at Ribbeck, which in turn reported to I. *Jagdkorps* under Generalmajor Joachim-Friedrich Huth at Treuenbritzen.

Steinhoff was assigned 29-year-old Major Erich Hohagen as *Kommandeur* of the first Me 262 *Gruppe* (III./JG 7) to be formed. A recipient of the Knight's Cross, Hohagen was regarded as one of the *Jagdwaffe's* true frontline veterans, having accumulated several thousand hours flying some 60 different types. He had also flown continuously on the Channel Front in 1940, during which time he had been credited with ten victories.

Major Erich Hohagen gazes at the camera from the cockpit of an Me 262 of III./EJG 2 at Lechfeld in the autumn of 1944. A tenacious fighter pilot who had been wounded and shot down on several occasions, he was a Knight's Cross holder who ended the war with 55 victories. Hohagen took over command of III./JG 7, having previously flown with the Me 262 training *Gruppe*, III./EJG 2, but like Steinhoff, his appointment would be relatively short-lived. He too went on to fly with JV 44

He was awarded the Knight's Cross on 5 October 1941 following his 30th victory. Hohagen was subsequently wounded over Russia on numerous occasions, and he returned to the West later in the war to take command of 7./JG 2 and then, on 7 April 1943, I./JG 27, operating in the defence of the Reich. However, he was shot down by Allied fighters over northern France on 1 June 1943, baling out wounded from his burning Bf 109. Following a period of hospitalisation, Hohagen was back in action as *Kommandeur* of I./JG 2 on 19 August 1943. Of his total of 55 victories gained from over 500 missions, 13 were four-engined bombers.

Following one air battle over the Western Front in the autumn of 1944, Hohagen had been forced to belly-land his stricken fighter in a small field. Aircraft and pilot had ploughed into a bank, and Hohagen smashed his head on the aircraft's reflector sight. A surgeon had later replaced a piece of his skull with plastic and pulled the skin back together. Even so, as Steinhoff later recalled, 'The two halves of his face no longer quite matched'.

Supposedly recovered from his injury, Hohagen was given command of the newly-formed Me 262 training *Gruppe* III./EJG 2 at Lechfeld in late 1944, before being assigned to lead III./JG 7. He was still troubled by headaches as a direct result of his many wounds, however, and found the task challenging.

III./JG 7 was assigned Oberinspektor Grote as its Technical Officer, while Leutnant Günther Preusker filled the role of Signals Officer. The former officer cadre of *Kommando Nowotny* was used to command the component *Staffeln*, with 9./JG 7 being led by Oberleutnant Joachim Weber – he had previously commanded 1./*Kdo. Nowotny* following the death of Oberleutnant Bley in a take-off accident at the end of October. Leutnant Franz Schall took over 10./JG 7 and Hauptmann Georg-Peter Eder led 11. *Staffel*.

In his memoirs, Johannes Steinhoff provides an insight into the early days of JG 7's existence;

'The first machines began to arrive. They came in sections on long railway trucks from the south of the Reich, and the mechanics, assisted by a team from the Messerschmitt works, started assembling them and shooting the cannon. By the end of November we were in the air, training in flights of three and in small formations.

'We could hardly have led a more unreal existence than we did in the first few weeks that were necessary to fly the aeroplanes in and get the complex machinery of a fighter group running smoothly. Not only were we left in peace, but our every wish – and a unit in the process of formation has a great many wishes – was complied with. We had time – time to play cards, time to talk, even time to go to the cinema, although air-raid warnings usually interrupted the performance.

'The city of Brandenburg was like the backdrop of a third-rate theatre. Houses lay in ruins, the gardens were untended and the peeling camouflage paint and shabby trams offered little temptation to hit town

Leutnant Joachim Weber (second from the right) served as *Staffelkapitän* of 9./JG 7. Although an experienced and accomplished jet pilot, he was killed in action flying against enemy bombers on 21 March 1945. Seen here with Weber is Oberleutnant Alfred Leitner (far left), who was a fighter controller attached to JG 7, Leutnant Günther Wegmann (centre left), *Kapitän* of 11./JG 7, and, at far right, JG 7 pilot Fahnenjünker-Feldwebel Joachim Zeller, formerly of JG 26, who would end the war with seven victories

Major Theodor Weissenberger was appointed *Kommandeur* of I./JG 7 in November 1944. A recipient of the Oakleaves to the Knight's Cross, much of his operational career had been spent in the Far North with JG 5. He also enjoyed great success with the unit after it was rushed to Normandy following the D-Day invasion. As the eventual successor to Steinhoff, Weissenberger was appointed *Kommodore* of JG 7. He proved equal to the task of leading the jet *Geschwader*, and did so until the cessation of hostilities. Weissenberger would end the war with 208 victories to his name

Oberleutnant Hans 'Specker' Grünberg, *Staffelkapitän* of 1./JG 7, was credited with 82 victories (including the destruction of seven Il-2s in three sorties in Russia in July 1943 whilst with 5./JG 3) during the course of 550 missions. He was awarded the Knight's Cross in July 1944

with our ration books and have a meal in a restaurant or a drink in a bar. We still had plenty to eat, plenty of brandy, champagne and red wine, and plenty of cigarettes and cigars.'

Following the establishment of III./JG 7, another *Gruppe*, I./JG 7, was formed on 27 November from pilots and personnel of the Bf 109-equipped II./JG 3 and placed under the command of Major Theodor Weissenberger.

Born in December 1914, Weissenberger joined the semi-autonomous *Zerstörerstaffel* 1.(Z)/JG 77, flying Bf 110s from Kirkenes over the Far North, before transferring to fly Bf 109s with II./JG 5 in the same theatre. By then he had accumulated 23 victories as a *Zerstörer* pilot, including eight Hurricane fighters. He was awarded the Knight's Cross on 13 November 1942 on the occasion of his 38th victory.

Weissenberger was made *Staffelkapitän* of 7./JG 5 in June 1943 and 6./JG 5 that September, following which he assumed command of II. *Gruppe* in late April 1944. In the interim he had received the Oakleaves to the Knight's Cross on 2 August 1943, by which time his tally had risen

Former *Zerstörer* pilot Leutnant Alfred 'Bubi' Schreiber flew with 9./JG 7, but he was an early loss for the *Geschwader* when his Me 262 crashed near Lechfeld on 26 November 1944

Oberleutnant Hans-Peter Waldmann took command of 3./JG 7 in November 1944, having been *Staffelkapitän* of 8./JG 3. The Knight's Cross holder and 134-victory ace would be killed in action during an operation mounted in adverse weather conditions on 18 March 1945

to 112. JG 5 moved to France to take part in operations over Normandy in June 1944, and he scored his 200th kill there on 25 July 1944.

Appointed as *Staffelkapitäne* of I./JG 7 were Oberleutnant Hans Grünberg, former *Staffelkapitän* of 5./JG 3 and a Knight's Cross holder with 77 victories to his credit for 1. *Staffel*, Oberleutnant Fritz Stehle, a former *Deutsche Lufthansa* and *Zerstörer* pilot from ZG 26 for 2. *Staffel*, and Oberleutnant Hans Waldmann, who had served as *Kapitän* of 4./JG 52 and 8./JG 3, for 3. *Staffel*. He too had been awarded the Knight's Cross, having downed 121 Soviet aircraft (including no fewer than 32 Il-2s) between August 1942 and May 1944.

While I./JG 7 commenced its formation period at Kaltenkirchen, III./JG 7 continued its training at both Briest and Lechfeld. But training was still proving dangerous, especially for pilots who were still grappling with flying a twin-engined aircraft powered by radical new technology that had to be handled carefully during take-off and landing.

On 26 November, the *Gruppe* suffered the loss of Leutnant Alfred 'Bubi' Schreiber of 9. *Staffel*, who died when his Me 262 crashed near

Lechfeld, while Oberfeldwebel Rudolf Alf of 1./JG 7, was killed while practising low-level flying near Fürstenfeldbrück. As Johannes Steinhoff told a British aviation journalist in 1954;

'Naturally, the flying qualities of the Me 262 were influenced by the high wing loading (280 kg per square metre) and the low thrust (850 kg per engine). We needed a 1200-metre runway, as the acceleration after take-off was slow because the aircraft had to be nursed during the first few minutes. At cruising speed – something over 800 km/h – the Me 262 handled well, except that the controls needed much force, particularly during violent manoeuvres – oil pressure controls, as used on modern jets, were then unknown.

'Similarly, though their absence nowadays is also unthinkable, we had to do without dive brakes, and this considerably limited our manoeuvrability, particularly as regards loops and turns. In order to reduce speed, it was neccesary to reduce power, which again, at high altitude, could lead to a compressor stall. The other weakness was the Junkers 004 turbines. Their blades could not withstand the temperatures sometimes reached, and this, together with faults in the induction system, often caused them to burn up. The life of these engines was, therefore, only 20 hours, and the accident rate was high.'

By the end of November, the *Geschwader* – now known by the new honour title of *Jagdgeschwader 7 'Nowotny'* – had only 11 of the 40 aircraft it was allocated. Even as more machines trickled in during December, a number were lost in bombing raids and through training crashes, while numerous others suffered damage from various causes – either accidental or as a result of enemy raids.

The starboard Jumo 004 engine of an Me 262 is fired up, jetting out a stream of white exhaust. Despite the tactical benefits of its superior performance, many of JG 7's pilots struggled to master the complexities of flying the Me 262. Its engines provided the biggest challenge, as they were prone to flame-outs, in-flight fires and stalling. Poor build quality also resulted in the engines being plagued by frequent parts failures

At least four precious pilots were also lost during December as a result of accidents, including the experienced Feldwebel Erwin Eichhorn, who was one of the original cadre of *Erprobungskommando* 262 that had transferred to *Kommando Nowotny*. His aircraft crashed and exploded on the runway at Lechfeld in full view of his fellow pilots following an engine failure. It was, in some ways, perhaps fortunate that inclement weather prevented further training by III./JG 7 until 20 December.

Johannes Steinhoff recalled;

'The fitting out of the group proceeded slowly. Assembling and flying in the aeroplanes was a time-consuming business, and there were hitches regarding parts and special components, as is often the case when you are introducing a new type. So it was all of six weeks before one had the feeling that a unit was taking shape – before, in other words, we were able to start proper formation training and I could at last report that, within limits, we "were ready for action".'

That action finally came on 2 December in the form of 'opening shots' by Leutnant Joachim Weber of 9./JG 7, who managed to shoot down an F-5 reconnaissance machine of the USAAF's 5th Photographic Reconnaissance Group (PRG) north of Munich, before being seen off by a P-51 from the 325th FG. The next day, former JG 5 pilot Oberfeldwebel August Lübking, serving with III./JG 7, claimed the destruction of a B-17 from the Fifteenth Air Force. Steinhoff added;

'December did not see much progress with the group. We were able to assemble enough aircraft in the hangars to bring the group staff and the Brandenburg wing up to strength, putting us in a position where we could risk our first outing. But the December weather seldom came up to the minimum conditions necessary to fly the aeroplanes in. There was usually low cloud, visibility was reduced by fog and the first snow showers swept across the airfield. Flying through cloud to find bombers was difficult enough anyway – in December it was impossible.'

Steinhoff's recollections are borne out by those of Oberfeldwebel Hermann Buchner, a former ground-attack pilot who had previously flown with 6./SG 2 on the Eastern Front. Having destroyed no fewer than 46 tanks, and been awarded the Knight's Cross in July 1944, he

An Me 262 of JG 7 photographed at Brandenburg-Briest in late January or early February 1945. Finished in a typical late-war paint scheme, the aircraft carries the running fox emblem of the *Geschwader* on its nose, and careful study of the image reveals a single chevron forward of the Balkenkreuz, denoting the aircraft's assignment to either the *Geschwader* Operations Officer or a *Gruppe* Adjutant

Engine failure claimed the life of Feldwebel Erwin Eichhorn (left), who was a jet 'veteran' from *Erprobungskommando* 262. His fighter crashed and exploded on the runway at Lechfeld in full view of his fellow pilots. Eichhorn is seen here with Heinz Lennartz in the summer of 1944, when both men served with the *Erprobungskommando* before moving to JG 7

23

subsequently joined 9./JG 7 in early December from Lechfeld and made the relatively rare transition from ground attack Fw 190s to Me 262s. He recalled;

'On 16 December, myself and three other pilots picked up four Me 262s from Obertraubling. The weather was very bad, so for several days we were unable to make the flight northwards. After a great deal of to-ing and fro-ing from the weather station, on Christmas Eve 1944 we

Another view of what appears to be the same Me 262 as seen in the photograph on page 23. The aircraft has probably been towed from its wooded dispersal at the edge of Brandenburg-Briest airfield and is seen here shortly before take-off on another sortie

An Me 262 of JG 7 taxies along the runway at Brandenburg-Briest in February 1945. It was at this point in the mission that the jet fighters were at their most vulnerable, being easy targets for strafing Allied fighters

Oberfeldwebel Hermann Buchner crouches on the surface of the upper wing to inspect the panelling of his Me 262A-1a 'White 7' of *Kommando Nowotny* at Lechfeld on 20 October 1944. Buchner was one of the very few ground-attack pilots who made the transition to the Me 262. He had been awarded the Knight's Cross in July 1944 for his service with SG 2 in Russia and Rumania

were given the go-ahead by the weathermen and could fly north on our own responsibility. I drew up a flight plan for a *Schwarm* of Me 262s to Brandenburg-Briest and started around midday. Because the weather had deteriorated en route, I decided to land the *Schwarm* on the factory airfield at Eger. The weather was extremely poor but the landing went smoothly. My *Kommandeur* at Briest was happy that I had the machines safely on the ground.'

Me 262s of III./JG 7 did manage to embark on a patrol near Magdeburg on 23 December and bounced a pair of F-5s of the US 7th PRG that were under escort from Mustangs of the 353rd FG – Oberfeldwebel Erich Büttner, a 'veteran' of *Ekdo. 262*, shot down one of the F-5s. In the encounter that ensued, the P-51s and Me 262s fought a low-level battle, during which Büttner and his fellow jet pilot, Oberfeldwebel Böckel, each claimed a Mustang. For their part, the Americans claimed two Me 262s but none of the 'victories' for either side can be verified. RAF Tempests also entered the fray against JG 7 on the 23rd when an aircraft of No 486 Sqn shot down the Me 262 piloted by Feldwebel Wilhelm Wilkenloh of 1./JG 7 near Schwabstadl.

A small core of the more potent jet pilots now began to emerge. On 29 December, Erich Büttner saw out the year by shooting down an RAF Mosquito reconnaissance aircraft, thought to have been flown by Flt Lt Olson of No 544 Sqn, while on the 31st Oberfeldwebel Baudach claimed a P-51 destroyed.

During the month of December, III./JG 7 had taken delivery of 41 Me 262s, while I. *Gruppe* received just two A-1as converted into two-seat trainers – this from a total monthly factory output of 114 aircraft, plus 17

Oberfeldwebel Hermann Buchner (right) is seen here in discussion with a fellow pilot of *Kommando Nowotny*, accompanied by a canine friend, at Lechfeld on 20 October 1944. Behind him, the starboard Jumo 004 engine on his Me 262 is being checked by mechanics. Buchner would more than prove his mettle as an Me 262 combat pilot in the opening months of 1945

repaired machines. Most of the balance had been assigned to I./KG(J) 54, the former bomber *Geschwader* that was converting to the Me 262 in the fighter defence role at Giebelstadt under the command of Oberstleutnant Volprecht Riedesel *Freiherr* zu Eisenbach.

The first morning of the new year saw the Luftwaffe launch a surprise low-level attack against 21 enemy airfields in North West Europe under the codename Operation *Bodenplatte*. A total of 41 *Gruppen*, drawn from ten *Jagdgeschwader* and one *Schlachtgeschwader*, as well as Me 262 and Ar 234 jet bombers from KG 51 and KG 76, were committed – in all a force of more than 900 aircraft. It was a monumental effort for the Luftwaffe to mount such an operation at this stage of the war, but it did not include the jet fighters of JG 7. They were needed for the defence of the capital and eastern cities.

Nevertheless, later in the day, as American heavy bombers returned from bombing German airfields in the Magdeburg area, Lt Franklin Young of the 4th FG, which was engaged in withdrawal support, intercepted the Me 262 flown by Leutnant Heinrich Lönnecker of 9./JG 7. He shot at it from a distance of 1000 metres, whereupon the jet nose-dived towards the earth and exploded southwest of Fassberg.

The new year also saw the III. *Gruppe Staffeln* disperse to their new operational bases, with 9./JG 7 going to Parchim, 10./JG 7 to Oranienburg and 11./JG 7, together with the *Gruppe Stab*, remaining at Brandenburg-Briest.

Aircraft losses suffered as a result of training accidents continued to dog the *Geschwader*. On New Year's Day, Unteroffizier Helmut Detjens of 10./JG 7 took off on his first operational flight against the enemy, accompanied by his *Staffelkapitän*, Oberleutnant Weber. As he climbed, Detjens began to experience landing gear problems and Weber throttled back and flew a wide circle as he urgently instructed the young Unteroffizier to land. Weber recorded;

'Despite clear visibility, Detjens wanted me to lead him back to the airfield. Instructions from the control tower were quite clear, and Detjens was brought back over his own field – he, however, did not realise this. Unfortunately, Detjens was not equal to this situation. He flew over the field and made a forced-landing beyond owing to fuel shortage. He claimed that his fuel state had altered after he was ordered to land, and that he did not realise quite how low on fuel he was. The crash can be attributed to Detjens' inexperience.'

Two weeks later, on 14 January, Helmut Detjens was lucky to remain alive when he was part of a very small force of Me 262s from 9. and 11./JG 7 sent up to assist the piston-engined fighters of JG 300 and JG 301 in their attempt to intercept more than 600 B-17s and B-24s, and their escort, despatched to bomb oil targets in northern Germany. Detjens was attacked by P-51s of the 353rd FG that were escorting the Liberators on their outward leg. It seems that the German pilot's aircraft received fire from a P-51 that riddled his machine from port to starboard. Detjens was forced to pull up sharply and bale out. A fellow pilot from 9./JG 7, Unteroffizier Heinrich Wurm, was pursued by three P-51s at high speed, and he eventually crashed into a field from a height of just 15 metres.

The following day I./JG 7 suffered its first loss when Unteroffizier Hans Werner was killed following an engine failure and a fire over Alveslohe, near Kaltenkirchen. Whether he was one of the '26 bomber personnel' that JG 7 reported numbered amongst its total strength of 546 men at this time is not known.

Unteroffizier Helmut Detjens of 10./JG 7 survived two dangerous incidents – a crash-landing in his Me 262 on New Year's Day 1945, which his *Staffelkapitän* attributed to 'inexperience', followed by an attack on his aircraft by a P-51 on 14 January in which he was forced to bale out

It was 'business as usual' for Hauptmann Georg-Peter Eder, leader of 11./JG 7 and by this time a recipient of the Oakleaves to his Knight's Cross, on 17 January when he claimed a B-17 shot down. This aircraft was almost certainly from the 351st BG, which had targeted the Paderborn marshalling yards that day. However, each victory seemed to bring with it a reversal, for on the 19th III. *Gruppe's* Unteroffizier Heinz Kühn was attacked over Ingolstadt by enemy aircraft. He baled out, but his parachute failed to open.

It had not been the notable start for JG 7 that Galland had hoped for. By this time, however, his aspirations were almost irrelevant, for he had been usurped as *General der Jagdflieger* by Göring, and on 23 January the *Reichsmarschall* officially announced Galland's dismissal and Oberst Gordon Gollob as his successor.

Now there was a change in the command of JG 7 too. Galland's close supporter, Johannes Steinhoff, suddenly found himself removed from his position as *Kommodore* of the *Geschwader* in favour of Theodor Weissenberger.

'The message they sent up to me with routine informality from the telex room was laconic', Steinhoff wrote in his memoirs, '"Oberst Steinhoff, Johannes, to hand over *Jagdgeschwader* 7 to Major W(eissenberger) with immediate effect. Further duties to be determined in due course. Signed, head of Personnel." The order said neither where I should report nor whom I now came under. All it told me was, "Beat it, at the double – we don't need you any more." What surprised me was that I felt no pain – only injured pride at being simply slung out like that. Nor did I feel as sad as when I had handed over JG 77, which I had commanded for years – then it had been like leaving a family. JG 7 was only eight weeks old, after all. The men who made it up had not had time to become a community – we had not yet started flying missions against the bombers.'

That was about to change.

CONSOLIDATION

With Steinhoff's departure to a brief period of oblivion and eventually to Adolf Galland's own controversial Me 262 unit *Jagdverband* 44, Theo Weissenberger set about reorganising the two *Gruppen* of JG 7. He envisaged a period of 20 days with which to fully 'reorganise' III./JG 7.

First to go was Erich Hohagen, who was replaced as *Kommandeur* of III. *Gruppe* on 24 January 1945 by Major Rudolf Sinner. An energetic and dedicated Austrian veteran, he had led 6./JG 27 over North Africa and the Mediterranean from June 1942 to May 1943, when he was appointed *Kommandeur* of IV./JG 27 in the Balkans. Later, Sinner served as *Kommandeur* of III./JG 54, during which time he was wounded in the thigh flying against B-17s over Berlin on 6 March 1944 and subsequently hospitalised. He then returned to JG 27, commanding I. *Gruppe* until the end of July 1944.

Rudolf Sinner recognised, as with all aircraft, that there were good and bad points with the Me 262;

'I was pleased and proud to be made responsible for the testing and operation in combat of a new, greatly promising and interesting weapon. With the advantages of increased speed and firepower, it was now possible to catch aerial targets – especially photo-reconnaissance aircraft – which, due to their superior performance compared to our piston-engined fighters, could not previously have been intercepted .

'Furthermore, we could attack heavily defended and escorted bomber formations with a considerable chance of success and less risk than was the case with piston-engined fighters. Alongside this, with repeated individual attacks by smaller numbers of combat-experienced pilots in Me 262s, we could seriously harass and confuse strong groups of enemy escort fighters and divert them from their planned defence of the bombers.

A semi-tracked Kettenkrad tow-tractor rumbles past a bicycle and a jet fighter – the Me 262A-1a of 37-victory ace Major Rudolf Sinner, *Gruppenkommandeur* of III./JG 7 – at Brandenburg-Briest in late January or early February 1945. Although this aircraft carries the tactical number 'Green 1', comparison with a jet featuring the same number on page 50 will reveal that although similar, the scheme on the Me 262 seen here has its camouflage 'stripe' running at opposite angles. It would appear that the aircraft is being serviced in readiness for its next mission

In the final months of the war, highly decorated ace Major Erich Rudorffer (seen here in Tunisia in 1942 while serving with II./JG 2) replaced Theodor Weissenberger as leader of I./JG 7

The Me 262A-1a of the *Geschwaderkommodore*, Major Theodor Weissenberger, rolls past the treeline at Brandenburg-Briest in February 1945. The aircraft carries the tactical number '4' in green on its nose, directly beneath the running fox emblem of the *Geschwader*. This machine also features extended horizontal bars either side of the fuselage Balkenkreuz and the blue and red Reich defence fuselage band

'However, there were a number of disadvantages. Flight duration was shorter and more dependent on altitude than in a piston-engined fighter. It was defenceless during take-off and landing, and the powerplants were more likely to suffer disturbance and had a shorter life than piston engines. Also, the demands upon airfield size, ground support, engineering, flight safety and tactical management were greater, and not adequately attended to in JG 7.

'Power dives in the Me 262, in contrast to other fighters, were only possible within a limited range. A sudden, dangerous pitch-up, with heavy control forces, was experienced if the highest permissable speed was exceeded. The engine starting procedure was more complicated and time-consuming than with piston-engined fighters. In summary, due to its advantages, the Me 262 was, despite these disadvantages, essentially better-suited to the defence of the Reich than our piston-engined fighters of the time. For field operations, it was less well-suited.'

Weissenberger's previous position at the head of I./JG 7 was taken by Major Erich Rudorffer, who was yet another very experienced officer. Flying since the French campaign of May 1940, during which he was an NCO pilot with JG 2, Rudorffer was awarded the Knight's Cross a year later for his 19 victories. He proved to be a potent adversary against the Western Allies, shooting down two Spitfires in one day over Dieppe in August 1942.

In November of that year he was appointed *Staffelkapitän* of 6./JG 2, and his unit moved to Tunisia, where he shot down eight British aircraft in 32 minutes on 9 February 1943. Six days later seven more enemy aircraft fell to his guns. Rudorffer subsequently took command of II./JG 2, but returned to France in April 1943. By the time he left the *Richthofen Geschwader* to take up his appointment as *Kommandeur* of the new IV./JG 54 in June, he had accumulated 74 victories.

Just weeks later, however, he was transferred to the East to take over II./JG 54 following the loss of that *Gruppe's* previous commander. Over Russia, Rudorffer excelled himself, and on one occasion claimed 13 Soviet machines shot down in 17 minutes. The Oakleaves to the Knight's Cross

Another view of Major Theodor Weissenberger's Me 262, seen here to the right. It is one of a pair of JG 7 jets preparing to take off from the concrete runway at Brandenburg-Briest in February 1945. Weissenberger's aircraft is identifiable by the extended horizontal bar forward of the fuselage Balkenkreuz. Note also that the forward part of the Jumo engine nacelle appears to have been changed since the photograph on page 29 was taken

The *Geschwader* emblem of *Jagdgeschwader* 7 – a light blue shield broken by a black diagonal band, superimposed with a white running fox. The emblem was usually seen on the nose of the *Geschwader's* jets, a little way forward of the cockpit. This photograph is something of a mystery as it is believed that the emblem seen here has been applied partially over the fairing of a camera housing, denoting an Me 262A-1a/U3 reconnaissance variant. This shot was almost certainly taken in the USA, which means that the aircraft must have been one of the small number of Me 262A-1a/U3s shipped over from Europe in July 1945, but the photographic records available suggest otherwise

followed on 11 April 1944 when his tally stood at 134 victories. There followed several more incidents of multiple kills in one day over the Eastern Front before he was awarded the Swords to Knight's Cross (the 126th such recipient) upon his 212th victory on 26 January 1945.

By the time he reached JG 7, Rudorffer had shot down 136 enemy aircraft in the East. He would end the war having clocked up more than 1000 missions, involving more than 300 encounters with the enemy, which resulted in ten four-engined bombers being destroyed. Rudorffer also baled out on no fewer than nine occasions, and was himself shot down 16 times.

A native of Lüneburg, Leutnant Rudolf Rademacher was a JG 54 veteran who had scored 90 victories flying under Walter Nowotny in Russia, before serving as a fighter instructor. He had been seriously wounded while flying an Fw 190 in a mission against American heavy bombers on 18 September 1944 and was awarded the Knight's Cross on 30 September for 81 victories. Recovered from his wounds, Rademacher joined 11./JG 7 on 30 January 1945.

With its 'backbone' of accomplished *Experten* such as Weissenberger, Eder, Sinner, Rudorffer, Schnörrer and Rademacher, *Jagdgeschwader* 7 was blessed with an enviable core of experienced pilots. Indeed, when Fritz Wendel from Messerschmitt's Technial Inspectorate visited the 'new' JG 7, he was impressed;

'Hauptmann Weissenberger, in collaboration with the *Kommandeur* of the III. *Gruppe*, Major Sinner, made excellent preparations for operational deployment. Ground control was perfected. "Safe flying" training was initiated – i.e. the pilots were trained in the use of radio aids for

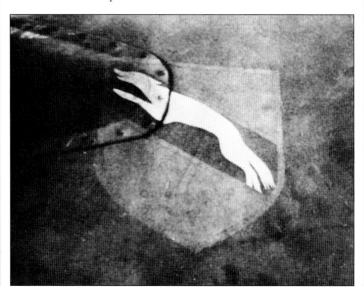

navigational purposes using the aircraft's radio equipment. Finally, formation flying in *Gruppe* strength was practised.'

Much of the improvement in formation flying was down to the efforts of Leutnant Preusker who worked hard to set up efficient air-ground communications systems using FuG 25a and FuG 16ZY transceivers for IFF (identification friend/foe), fighter control and homing, while Leutnant Richard Frodl oversaw the technical aspects of the entire *Geschwader*, having replaced Hauptmann Streicher.

Yet practice did not always make perfect, for on 14 January Oberfähnrich Hans-Joachim Ast of 10./JG 7 was killed when his jet suffered a mechanical failure whilst in flight and crashed near Crivitz from a height of 4500 metres.

Furthermore, while JG 7's senior personnel may have been strengthened, according to Allied radio intercept intelligence, the supply of new aircraft was still patchy. At the end of January, I./JG 7 reported only one serviceable Me 262A-1 and a sole Me 262B-1 trainer – just one new aircraft had been added during the month. A senior British intelligence officer who read the report noted sardonically, 'This is the best they can do after four weeks. In fact they have one less aircraft than eight weeks ago'.

I. *Gruppe* Technical Officer Leutnant Frodl, who had arrived from his position as commander of the *Kampfsstaffel* of the tactical and weapons evaluation unit *Jagdgruppe 10* to take over from Leutnant Karsten, lamented;

'When I arrived at Kaltenkirchen on 8 January 1945 as the advanced detachment of the technical section conditions were catastrophic. The only member of the flying personnel there was "Specker" Grünberg. Three jets sat in a corner of the airfield, and these were non-flyable because there were no replacement parts to be found and no jet engine workshop. Workers from a concentration camp were busy extending the runway, and if that wasn't enough, the fog was so thick that you couldn't see your hand in front of your face. We needed weeks before the field was halfway in shape for conducting flight operations.'

Leutnant Rudolf Rademacher joined 11./JG 7 with 81 victories scored over the Eastern Front. He accounted for four P-51s and an RAF fighter shot down while flying the Me 262A, as well as eleven four-engined bombers

Alarmstart! The Me 262A-1a of Major Rudolf Sinner, *Gruppenkommandeur* of III./JG 7, takes off from Brandenburg-Briest on another sortie against incoming Allied bombers. Note the matching continued lines of colour demarcation running over the nose and the engine nacelle, shown to good effect in this view

Three Me 262s of JG 7 lined up on a concrete-surfaced dispersal point at Brandenburg-Briest in late January or early February 1945. All three machines have different paint finishes. The nearest aircraft is camouflaged in a fairly common late war mottle, but it appears to have no tactical number or *Geschwader* emblem, possibly indicating a newly delivered machine. The centre aircraft is finished in a striped scheme similar to that seen on Major Rudolf Sinner's Me 262, while the furthest jet boasts an overall dark green finish with a lower demarcation line and lighter undersurfaces. The two jets nearest to the camera also have the rarer solid white Hakenkreuz on their tails

The British assessment, however, is at odds with total German delivery statistics, which list 148 Me 262 fighters as having been issued to the Luftwaffe, with another 14 repaired in January 1945 – a total of 162. Of these, 15 machines went to I./JG 7 and 11 to III./JG 7. The rest were delivered to the various other jet units forming up at the time – most going to I. and III./KG(J) 54, with small numbers to the *Industrie Schutz Schwärme*, the experimental nightfighter detachment *Kommando Welter*, III./KG(J) 6, the *Flieger Überführungs Geschwader*, IV./EKG 1, NAG 6, and another experimental detachment under Professor Gladenbeck.

Combat sorties seemed to have been sporadic at this time, and as with the previous month, the isolated victories were marred by losses. A day after joining JG 7, Rudolf Rademacher claimed a Spitfire shot down near Braunschweig on 1 February, although the only Allied loss in the area was a Tempest V. However, a week earlier, Oberfähnrich Karl Schnurr (a fellow pilot in Rademacher's III. *Gruppe*) was lost when his jet apparently dived vertically into the ground whilst on a test flight close to Lübz, in the Mecklenburg area. His Me 262 had just been fitted with two new engines and a generator.

The paucity in operations at this time is reflected in the fact that the Chief of the Luftwaffe's Operations Staff had to give 'permission' to III./JG 7 to engage enemy reconnaissance aircraft and fighters. It seems the Me 262 was still too precious a resource to lose in the testing battle against the Allied bombers. Certainly, the *Gruppe* had just 17 aircraft at this point, with another ten promised to arrive soon, although on 2 February a jet was lost in a landing accident at Neuburg.

The following day, despite the fact that III./JG 7 reported itself still not completely ready for operations, the unit embarked upon what was its first major operation in any 'strength'. Amongst the targets attacked by the USAAF on the 3rd were the marshalling yards at Berlin-Tempelhof, which were bombed by B-24s from the 2nd Air Division.

Some 116 Liberators reached the target, but the small force of Me 262s made its mark. Leutnant Rademacher claimed two 'B-17s' shot down, but it is more likely these were B-24s. Oberleutnant Weber of 9./JG 7 and Oberleutnante Wegmann and 'Quax' Schnörrer of 11./JG 7 also claimed a '*Viermot*' (bomber) each. Hauptmann Eder, leading 11./JG 7, is believed to have shot down two P-47s, while Unteroffizier Anton Schöppler, who had flown with I./JG 5 over Normandy, claimed a P-51. The Americans lost 23 B-17s, two B-24s and seven P-51s during their raid that day, with the only claim against a jet being made by a Mustang pilot of the 364th FG who reported damaging a Me 262 south of Gardelegen.

On 5 February 1945, Göring overturned the OKL's earlier edict of 1 February and decreed that until the new EZ 42 gyroscopic gunsight had been delivered, JG 7 (and all other Me 262 units) was to only attack heavy bomber formations utilising similar close-range massed attack tactics as used by the piston-engined fighters of the *Sturm Gruppen*.

For many years, German fighter aircraft had been largely equipped with simple Revi 12 or 16 reflector gunsights. These required the pilot to estimate the angle of deflection to the target according to combat conditions, but, in reality, this could only be done with any degree of accuracy when engaging at short range and/or when attacking from a central position with minimum deflection. As the range and intensity of enemy defensive firepower improved, so it became harder for a fighter pilot to attack a bomber from a sharp angle at close range. A sight was needed that would allow greater flexibility by allowing a pilot to attack from virtually any position at a longer range.

It was envisaged that the EZ 42, under development by the Askania and Carl Zeiss companies, would allow a pilot to fire at an airborne target without having to make allowance for the rounds' movement from fixed guns built into the longitudinal axis of the carrying aircraft. When approaching a target, a pilot had to ensure that he continuously twisted the range-finding button on the aircraft's control column so that the growing target was permanently encapsulated in the dial, as well as making sure that the cross-wire was contained within the target-circle on the target. The precise angle of deflection was obtained within two seconds. Accuracy could be guaranteed to within 15 per cent of the angle of deflection in the longitudinal direction of the enemy and 10 per cent perpendicularly.

On 9 February, I./JG 7 is known to have had just 12 aircraft on strength. In an effort to rectify this situation, that same day the

Unteroffizier Anton Schöppler is believed to have joined 3./JG 7 from I./JG 5, and he was subsequently transferred to 11. *Staffel*. He shot down a Mustang while flying an Me 262 on 3 February 1945

The EZ 42 gyroscopic gunsight, manufactured by Askania and Carl Zeiss, was intended to be widely fitted into the Luftwaffe's Me 262s in order to improve accuracy in deflection shooting, but pilots who flew machines so fitted found the equipment problematic to use

Reichsmarschall ordered the two Me 262 *Industrieschwärme* (factory defence flights) to be disbanded and their personnel and aircraft transferred to JG 7 in order to reinforce it. Whether this ever actually happened is open to conjecture.

Also on 9 February, the Eighth Air Force returned to northern and central Germany, this time striking at oil, transport and airfield targets including Magdeburg, Lützkendorf and Paderborn. In the Berlin area, a few Me 262s from III./JG 7 attacked B-17s, with Leutnant Rademacher claiming two shot down and Hauptmann Eder and Oberleutnant Wegmann being credited with one apiece. Leutnant Schnörrer also claimed a P-51. Yet such were the debilitating odds stacked against the Luftwaffe by this stage that in reviewing the German fighter response to the American raid on 9 February, against which only 67 single-engined fighters were deployed, the Chief of the Luftwaffe's Operations Staff lamented 'that the employment of such a small number of aircraft is purposeless, and must be regarded as a mistake'.

The next day, *General der Jagdflieger* Oberst Gordon Gollob received orders from OKL to redesignate the Fw 190A-8-equipped IV./JG 54 at Neumünster under Major Hermann Staiger as the new II./JG 7 in preparation for it being re-equipped with Me 262s. Under this directive, the 13., 14. and 15. *Staffeln* of IV./JG 54 would form the component elements of II./JG 7, while 16./JG 54 was to be placed at the disposal of Generalleutnant Galland with the aim of creating a new *Staffel*, not to test the Me 262 in combat, but rather as a jet training unit for NCO pilots. Happily for Galland, however, OKL's orders seem not to have been adhered to.

A short while later, between 23-25 February, Galland discussed personnel, aircraft and equipment requirements with officers from the staff of the Luftwaffe's Chief of General Staff, *General der Flieger* Karl Koller. Galland proposed the creation of a sophisticated 'self-supportive' unit with a nominal strength of 16 Me 262s and 15 pilots, with appropriate technical and ground support. Koller authorised the immediate establishment of what would become almost a 'rival' unit to JG 7 – *Jagdverband* 44 (see *Osprey Aviation Elite Units 27 - Jagdverband 44* for further details).

In the meantime, on 12 February – a deadline set by Göring – III./JG 7 finally declared itself fully operational with 50 aircraft. Two days later, the USAAF sent another large raid comprised of nearly 1300 B-17s and B-24s, escorted by 881 fighters, to 17 assorted targets including Dresden, Prague, Brüx, Pilsen, Chemnitz and Magdeburg. Some bombers were forced to return early and were intercepted by several Me 262s from I. *Gruppe* and 11./JG 7. Leutnant Rademacher, Unteroffiziere Schöppler and Günther Engler (who had joined JG 7 from JG 3) all accounted for a bomber each, and a single Me 262 was lost when its pilot was forced to bale out after having been attacked by the fighter escort.

Rademacher claimed again on the 16th when III./JG 7 took on a formation of P-51s in the Hannover area. His victim is believed to have been a Mustang of the 325th FG.

Despite victories in the air, accidents on the ground were still the curse of JG 7. In late January, a jet being delivered to the *Geschwader* was crashed by a ferry pilot when he became lost and his fuel ran out. Worse

Leipheim-built Me 262A-1a Wk-Nr. 110800 'Yellow 7' was used by Unteroffizier Günther Engler of 3./JG 7 to shoot down an American heavy bomber during the USAAF raid on targets in central Germany on 14 February 1945. The jet was coded 'Yellow 9' during this mission, however. Engler would eventually surrender to the British at Fassberg in this aircraft – coded 'Yellow 7'

was to come, for in the five days between 2-6 February, three Me 262s were lost or damaged due to accidents or engine fires – an increasingly common occurrence. An unteroffizier was killed in a crash due to engine failure on 9 February, and two days later Major Ludwig Grözinger of 11./JG 7 also crashed near Lechfeld as a result of the same problem. Grözinger was a former bomber pilot who had flown He 111s with KG 53 over England in 1940 and on the Eastern Front, where he was appointed *Staffelkapitän* of 3./KG 53 and later led IV./KG 53. During his career in the East, Grözinger had made some 80 successful bombing attacks on Soviet railway stations, earning him a Knight's Cross in November 1942.

On 15 February I./JG 7 lost Unteroffizier Hans Werner when his aircraft caught fire south of Kaltenkirchen soon after take-off. Five days later Feldwebel Germar Nolte was killed when his Me 262 crashed south of Lamderdingen, while another of the unit's jets crashed at Lechfeld and was destroyed the next day. On the 25th, Oberleutnant Böhm died in his aircraft when it crashed on a training flight near Deberndorf.

In a document dated 19 February 1945, which, to some extent, contradicts reality, Fritz Wendel appraised the training of JG 7;

'The pilots of I. *Gruppe* (*Kommandeur* Major Rudorffer (212 kills)) have, in principle, all converted to the Me 262. What is lacking so far is training in close formation flying and low-level navigation (using FuG 16 Z and FuG 25 a). Up to 9 February, the *Gruppe* had 12 aircraft. Assuming normal output of the Brandenburg-Briest assembly centre, the *Gruppe* should be operational by the end of this month.

'The last, i.e. II. *Gruppe*, will then be re-equipped as quickly as possible. Its operational status depends on aircraft availability and pilot conversion at Lechfeld. Since, however, the *Ergänzungsgruppe* at Lechfeld has only four airworthy aircraft out of 19 due to lack of engines, conversion training will not be able to keep pace with aircraft production.

'The first large operation has been well prepared by Hauptmann Weissenberger. Complete success is guaranteed by the excellent training of pilots. However, after the first missions, availability of operational aircraft will go down due to problems in supplying spare parts for airframe and engines – the supply depot at Jüterbog having insufficient stocks.

Immediate improvement is necessary. Possibly an engine shop will have to be set up at JG 7's base.

'Nearly all III. *Gruppe* aircraft had to be retro-fitted at the distribution centre. It was discovered that the installation manuals were wrong in several instances. The control column's neutral position has to be adjusted by 1 degree, 30 mins. No mention of this is made. In the "down" position, elevator angle should be 20 degrees, whilst it is actually 26 degrees.

'Considerably more pushrods, in particular for the rudder, are being supplied than required for replacement according to the manufacturer's drawings.

'The pilots, especially Hauptmann Weissenberger, are enthusiastic about the adjustable control column. It is generally believed that the improved manoeuvrability offered by the new column will increase the kill-rate against enemy fighters. The actuating lever should, however, be larger with position indicators for "take-off", "landing" and "flight". On many (Leipheim) aircraft, control surfaces were wrongly set. Differences of up to six degrees were found with rudder and ailerons.

'III./JG 7 aircraft were later fitted with heating. There are complaints about excessive cabin heat. Even with the heater closed, the temperature is too high for the time of year. Attention, therefore, should be drawn to the need to modify the air vents. The new vents would have to be fitted before the start of the warm season. The heated windscreen panels have cracked repeatedly, particularly shortly after having been switched off. The obvious cause is insufficient strength of the canopy against heat caused by tension. I have arranged for the disconnection of heated panels on a few aircraft. They will now be heated by hot air from the heating system.

'There have been cases of the nosewheel locking at right angles during landings on snow or ice-covered runways. When do we get the offset wheel fork? Why is mass production still being delayed? The reason given, namely that the new fork will only be introduced with the hydraulic shimmy-damper, is wrong, since it is most likely that no shimmy-damper will be necessary with the new fork.'

On 17 February, Oberst Gollob was able to report that the new II./JG 7 had commenced training following the order for the *Gruppe's* establishment a week earlier. Mean- while, at least three pilots from 9./JG 7, led by *Staffelkapitän* Hauptmann Georg Peter Eder, were scrambled from Parchim the same day on an '*Alarmstart*' to intercept what were probably incoming Lancasters from RAF Bomber Command operating in daylight against the Ruhr. Eder was accompanied by fellow Knight's Cross holder Oberfeldwebel Büch- ner, as well as Oberfeldwebel Hel- mut Zander. The small formation of Me 262s sighted the bombers south of Bremen and the Luftwaffe pilots prepared to make an attack on the formation from the rear. As they did

Me 262A-1a Wk-Nr. 111588 'White 5' of 11./JG 7 is serviced close to what appears to be a bomb crater at Brandenburg-Briest in late January or early February 1945. Note the unusual markings on the tail assembly and rudder

so, they were greeted by massed defensive fire from the bombers' gunners. Hermann Buchner recalled;

'The Me 262 reached us too late. The fighter was years ahead of its time from the point of view of its technology. Of course, there were shortcomings, but with more time and sufficient operational experience, these could have been eliminated. The main problem was that the crews had to work out new methods of attack, learning how best to engage enemy bombers at such high closing speeds.

'In an attack, firing time was greatly reduced as we reached the target ridiculously fast. I accounted for most of my claims by basically approaching from the rear. Of course, you had to fly through the escort. This was often difficult in the Fw 190, but was no problem with the Me 262. With a sufficient number of Me 262s deployed, the escort fighters had no chance of preventing us from making firing passes at the bombers. Attacks began at a distance of 500 metres, and you had to overcome your basic survival instincts and press on through the bombers' defensive fire.

'It was very important to target the tail gunner's turret, centring the gunsight on the muzzle flash and smoke of the machine guns. If the rear gunner could be taken out, success was much more certain. And when the R4M rocket was introduced, our chances were further improved.'

On this mission, however, Hauptmann Eder's jet was hit and his left engine and wing immediately started to burn.

'The aircraft was beyond saving', he later recalled. 'Baling out after being hit was nothing new for me. I had already gone through this exercise 16 times before. I jettisoned the canopy, pulled the nose up to lose speed, disconnected my helmet lead and stood up in the seat. The slipstream took care of the rest. I may have struck either the fuselage or the tail. In any case, I suddenly felt a terrible pain in my leg and head. I let myself fall to perhaps 2500 metres and then pulled the parachute release handle.'

After landing, Eder was taken to hospital suffering from a broken leg and head injuries. He would not fly operationally again until April. The loss of one of its most experienced unit commanders was a severe blow to JG 7. Eder's place was taken by Oberleutnant Günther Wegmann.

Elsewhere, two more precious Me 262s were destroyed in accidents on the ground, Oberfeldwebel Hans Clausen being killed when his aircraft failed to take off, and a second jet falling victim to yet another engine fire, although its pilot managed to escape. Three more Me 262s were damaged.

As if Eder's predicament and the loss of three aircraft were not bad enough, the next day, 18 February, saw the loss of another jet, but this time it was the machine of the *Kommodore*, the recently promoted Major Weissenberger. While on a routine flight at 8000 metres, Weissenberger's aircraft suffered the, by now, all too familiar fire to the left engine. Initially, he decided to try and glide back down to earth, but the ferocity of the fire quickly brought the wing to breaking point and so Weissenberger baled out of his stricken Me 262 at 6500 metres. As he drifted downwards, he watched the aircraft smash into the ground and burst into flames northwest of Brandenburg. The ace landed a little later in a forest clearing. He too was hospitalised, suffering from concussion.

Elsewhere, another aircraft, belonging to I./JG 7, was damaged at Kaltenkirchen.

A groundcrewman closes the canopy of Leipheim-built Me 262A-1a Wk-Nr. 111892 of III./JG 7 at Brandenburg-Briest in the early spring of 1945. Note the last three digits of the Werknummer visible on the tail assembly and the blue and red defence of the Reich identification band on the rear fuselage, adorned with III. *Gruppe's* vertical white bar

Some 15 jets of III./JG 7 attacked P-51s of the US 479th FG near Potsdam on 21 February. The Mustangs quickly recovered, turning into the Me 262s, which quickly outclimbed the US fighters. The German pilots then performed a second strike from above and to the rear, their opponents reporting;

'This kept up for three or four breaks, neither us or Jerry being able to get close enough for a shot. Each time we would break they would climb straight ahead, outdistancing us. The Jerry pilots were aggressive and experienced. They were not caught in a turn, and if caught in such a position would roll out and climb away. It was impossible to catch or climb with them.

'The fighting took place from 12,000 ft up to 26,000 ft. A P-51 cannot climb with the jet, particularly if it has an initial altitude advantage. However, a P-51 can out-turn the jet. Indeed, Red Flight managed to out-turn the jets after being bounced without having to first drop their tanks. The jet is faster on a straight and level run. Its rate of roll was excellent, but its turning radius was poor. Their job seemed to have been to force us to drop our tanks so that we would have to leave. We were over southwest Berlin, and we found the expenditure of gas while attempting to close very heavy. It was necessary to use full power all the time. The jets flew excellent formation, and never allowed themselves to be caught in a bad position.'

This encounter ended without loss to either side.

On 22 February the combined Allied Air Forces launched Operation *Clarion*, which was a major bombing offensive aimed at knocking out the remaining German transport and communications system. Nearly 9000 aircraft, operating from bases in England, France, Holland, Belgium and Italy, attacked over 650,000 square kilometres of territory, targeting railways, bridges, ports and roads – the US Eighth Air Force alone targeted 33 transport junctions.

This day may have seen the first 'maximum effort' on the part of JG 7, which utilised all its available aircraft. In its Daily Situation Report, the OKL Operations Staff recorded, '34 Me 262s of JG 7 took off but were not able to engage the heavy bombers as they were immediately involved in intensive actions with enemy fighters. Only five enemy aircraft were shot down.'

OKL's figure is at odds with the claims made by its pilots. Oberleutnant Wegmann, now leading 11./JG 7 following Eder's demise, claimed a P-51, while Gefreiter Hermann Notter of the *Geschwader Stab* was credited with the destruction of two B-17s, following which he was forced to belly-land near Stade. Finally, Oberfeldwebel Buchner shot down a P-51 of the 364th FG. I./JG 7 was also operational, but only just. It managed to sortie two machines from Brandenburg-Briest, one flown by the *Staffelkapitän* of 3./JG 7, Oberleutnant Hans-Peter Waldmann, and the other by his wingman, Oberfähnrich Günther Schrey, formerly of JG 3. Waldmann claimed two P-51s destroyed around midday near Oschersleben flying Me 262 '1' during a 66-minute sortie that ended with both jets landing at Kaltenkirchen.

As was increasingly becoming the norm for JG 7, these successes came at a price. Oberfeldwebel Helmut Baudach of 10. *Staffel* (a veteran of *Erprobungskommando* 262 and *Kommando Nowotny*) struck his head against his aircraft's tail as he baled out not far from Schönewald. He survived the incident, but died a few days later. It was another heavy blow to the unit, and the Luftwaffe in general, as there were few pilots in the frontline that had the same level of experience in the Me 262 as Baudach.

Oberfeldwebel Heinz-Berthold Mattuschka of 11./JG 7 escaped with his life when he too baled out of his jet fighter near Hagenow. Eight more jets were lost in accidents on the 22nd at Döberitz, Stade, Kaltenkirchen and Lärz.

A widely-recognised vulnerability of the Me 262 were the moments when it prepared to take off or when it approached for landing. At such moments, greater lengths of time and distance were required than for conventional fighter aircraft. The jet also required a longer period of time to start its engines, and this would frequently have to be done in the open,

Oberfeldwebel Helmut Baudach had previously flown with both *Erprobungskommando* 262 and *Kommando Nowotny* prior to being assigned to 10./JG 7. He was fatally injured as he baled out of his jet fighter on 22 February 1945 following a clash with P-51s near Schönewald

thus exposing the Me 262 to the very real threat of attack from increasingly numerous and ever-confident Allied fighters.

22 February also saw the OKL take the precautionary measure of ordering III./JG 3 to make available to transfer one *Staffel* each for Brandenburg-Briest, Parchim and Oranienburg airfields. 'At this point', the OKL diary noted somewhat oddly, 'III./JG 7 will be free for operations.'

Some 345 B-17s of the Eighth Air Force's 1st Air Division struck at two oil refineries at Hamburg on the 24th, and as they did so, 10. and 11./JG 7 attempted to intercept them in the airspace between the city and Lüneburg. Despite the fact that the P-51 escort successfully screened the formation from attack, Leutnant Rademacher put in a claim for a Flying Fortress and Leutnant Weber for a Mustang.

The following day the 1. *Jagddivision* reported that ten Me 262s were active from JG 7 but no details are known. Three days later, Rademacher struck again and raised his personal tally to 90 victories when he brought down a B-24 in the Halle-Leipzig area – one of two lost from the 314 Liberators of the 2nd Air Division sent to bomb Halle marshalling yards.

On the last day of the month, III./JG 7 mounted 22 fruitless sorties directed at heavy bombers operating between Braunschweig and Brandenburg. Any sense of ineffectiveness would have been worsened by news that three more *Gruppe* aircraft had been damaged in accidents.

In late February, with Allied fighters now virtually ruling the skies over Germany and losses continuing to mount, the OKL proposed that German fighters should only attack lone bombers straggling behind a formation.

Also on 28 February, an earlier spectre came back to haunt the OKL Operations Staff in the form of an order from the *Führer* that all available aircraft in the West should be used in bombing and strafing operations against the American thrust through the Reydt-Köln area. Furthermore, 'The additional employment of III./JG 7 and I./KG(J) 54 on bombing operations as a precautionary measure is being considered. The Chief of Staff of the Luftwaffe expresses serious misgivings at the employment of the two fighter *Gruppen* as fighter-bombers, as a build-up of the Me 262 fighter *Geschwader* for the defence of the Reich will thus be delayed and undermined. The *Reichsmarshall* must be informed and come to a decision'.

February 1945 had seen 25 new Me 262s delivered to I./JG 7, ten to II./JG 7 and seven to III./JG 7. This was out of a total of 212 new jets squeezed from the factories, with another 12 repaired. Curiously, the 'winning' unit in terms of taking delivery of new machines was not JG 7 – which was tasked with defending the critical area around the German capital – but rather KG(J) 54, the bomber *Geschwader* converted to fly jet fighters. This may have been attributable to the measure of influence that bomber officers such as Generalmajor Dietrich Peltz, commander of IX.(J) *Fliegerkorps* (which also oversaw the activities of the similarly converted III./KG(J) 6), exerted over tactical affairs at this time, or perhaps the fact that bomber pilots experienced in twin-engined aircraft were more adept at handling the Me 262 than young, hastily trained and largely inexperienced fighter pilots.

Whatever the case, *Jagdgeschwader* 7 would need every single pilot and every single aircraft it could acquire, for the coming month would test the unit's mettle to its limit.

EXPERIMENTATION

Early in January 1945, four Me 262s were delivered to an experimental air-to-air bombing unit designated *Kommando Stamp*. This was led by Knight's Cross holder Major Gerhard Stamp, a former bomber pilot who had flown Ju 88s over the Mediterranean during 1942 with I./LG 1. Later, he pioneered *Wilde Sau* single-seat nightfighter operations, before taking command of I./JG 300, which provided high-altitude cover for the heavily-armoured Fw 190-equipped *Sturmgruppen* in the defence of the Reich.

In June 1944, at Merzhausen airfield, Stamp had a chance meeting with a professor from the technical college at Braunschweig. The professor asked Stamp to test a barometric fuse that he had developed – he promptly dropped the device from high altitude the next time he was airborne over the airfield. As a direct result of this flight, Stamp began formulating ideas on how to knock down B-17s and B-24s en masse using fused bombs dropped from fighters. And as early as November 1944, he had recognised

Major Gerhard Stamp (right) had flown Ju 88s with I./LG 1 prior to transferring to the Jagdwaffe to fly in the defence of the Reich with JG 300. He believed that the Me 262 could 'fill expectations' and win the air war for Germany. He was later given his own *Kommando*, which he used to test the jet fighter in a series of air-to-air bombing experiments. He is seen here conversing with Major Wolfgang Späte, *Kommodore* of JG 400

the tactical potential of the Me 262 in this role. In a report prepared for senior commanders that month he wrote;

'The main question needing to be addressed is that of the potential benefits which could be achieved by the latest types of fighter aircraft whose operational use has been proposed, but which will not be available in large numbers for some time. The problem of the air defence of the Reich is, at present, not so much a question of how to concentrate our fighter strength but of how to effectively attack the enemy's fighter cover, and thus be able to strike at the bombers.

'As far as the performance of the Bf 109 and Fw 190 against enemy types is concerned, it has become apparent that to achieve any decisive rise in success, the ratio of escort fighters to *Sturmjäger* would have to be increased to at least four-to-one to combat the enemy fighter cover alone. At present, not only are too few enemy aircraft being shot down, but losses inflicted by escorting enemy fighters are so high that our units are being drained of their resources.

'The solution to the problem of successful defence lies in counter-action against enemy fighters, which are superior in both numbers and performance. These considerations lead to the conclusion that a change in the air situation over the Reich is not possible with the forces presently available. If, on the other hand, the Luftwaffe could operate in sufficient strength with these new aircraft types, then we might beat the enemy's fighters, and thus bring about a change in the whole situation. The Me 262 is capable of fulfilling these expectations.'

The idea of using the Me 262 in the air-to-air bombing role had originated with Oberst Berndt von Brauchitsch, *Reichsmarschall* Göring's Chief Adjutant. Von Brauchitsch believed that such tactics would break up a tight-flying bomber formation, thus breaking down the density of its combined defensive firepower, and thereby producing favourable conditions for attack by German fighters.

However, the problem facing Luftwaffe tacticians was that their piston-engined fighters needed too much time to attain the required height for bomb-dropping. This meant that although well within sight of the enemy, the fighter units waiting to exploit the weakness in the bombers' defensive capability caused by bomb-dropping were forced for their own safety to hold back their attack until the bomb-dropping had actually taken place. Nor were German aircraft equipped with a suitable bombsight for such operations, which meant that ordnance had to be dropped according to the pilot's visual estimation.

It was also found that the Allied fighter escort tended to react immediately by despatching sufficient numbers of aircraft to a higher altitude to deal with the threat. Furthermore, even when dropped, it was discovered that the bomb types used had insufficient blast effect, and that their time fuses produced delays of varying, and thus unreliable, periods.

However, by deploying Me 262s fitted with jettisonable weapons containers loaded with semi armour-piercing bombs (these were equipped with time fuses designed to produce the maximum possible blast effect), von Brauchitsch believed that the jet's superior speed would overcome all the earlier disadvantages faced by piston-engined fighters.

By 8 January 1945, *Kommando Stamp* was based at Lärz with four aircraft on strength (although six had been allocated) and at least five

Like Gerhard Stamp, Oberleutnant Herbert Schlüter had flown defence of the Reich missions with I./JG 300 before being assigned to *Kommando Stamp*. 'The purpose of the unit' Schlüter recalled 'was to bomb bombers'. He subsequently joined the *Stab* of JG 7

pilots – Oberfeldwebel Hanns-Werner 'Hanschen' Gross (formerly of 1. and 4./JG 300), Oberfeldwebel Eberhard Gzik (formerly of 2./JG 300), Oberleutnant Georg Seip, Oberleutnant Herbert Schlüter and Feldwebel Gustav Sturm (from JG 51).

Like Gross and Gzik, Schlüter had been a fighter pilot with JG 300, flying Bf 109s with I. *Gruppe* on escort missions alongside Gerhard Stamp for the *Sturmjäger* of that *Geschwader* in the defence of the Reich. In September 1944, he was transferred to *Erprobungskommando* 262 at Lechfeld for training on the Me 262.

'We were to be trained on the Me 262 and transferred to Lechfeld', Schlüter recalled. This was a joyous occasion, since flying the Me 262 was a dream for me, as well as all the others. The numerical superiority of the Americans was too great. The performance of our Bf 109Gs was inferior to the much-faster Mustangs, which could break off combat at will.

'This was an extremely difficult time for us. The daily strain was hard to take. We were on the defensive and were "the hunted". For this reason, I was happy to be transferred. Finally, we would have the chance to fly a superior aircraft, and show the *"Amis"*how we could do it better.'

Later, Schlüter received orders to transfer to *Kommando Nowotny*, but before joining the unit, he received replacement orders instructing him to report to Unterschlauersbach, where he was to train pilots from JG 3 for conversion to the Me 262. However, in early January, he received some further, unexpected orders. 'I was transferred to *Kommando Stamp* at Rechlin-Lärz. Purpose of the unit – to bomb bombers'.

In addition to its pilots, the *Kommando* was assigned 40 other military and civilian personnel and weapons specialists who acted in a technical and support capacity, including two professors from the technical colleges at Braunschweig and Brünn and four female communications specialists. The unit's headquarters was set up in a *Reichsbahn* train located behind some aircraft hangars on the edge of the Müritzkanal. The unit had the benefit of a number of sleeping coaches, the dining car and another coach assigned for radio and technical equipment. As Stamp recalled;

'I admired both the elegant and powerful-looking design of the Me 262, and I was conscious that I was witnessing a new era in flying. Nosewheels and jet engines were completely new to me – the latter required a completely different pattern of take-off and landing procedures. The high cruising speed, previously not experienced, required a complete change in the "feeling" of time and distance. Compared to other aircraft, it represented a completely new style and feel of flying – no noise and no vibration in the air.

'From an operational point of view, I was sure that the aircraft could and would do what I had proposed, and what I had now been given the opportunity to do – to take two 250-kg bombs, climb to 9000 metres, drop them into closed bomber formations, split them and create better attack conditions for our conventional fighter pilots.'

Tactically, Stamp planned to use four Me 262 bomb-carriers for an attack on an enemy bomber *pulk*, with each aircraft initially carrying one weapon, although some trials were later attempted with two in accordance with Stamp's intentions. The jets would fly echeloned back 10-15 degrees in a loose line astern formation, with about 28 metres between each aircraft, abreast of the bomber formation and at the same altitude. Each pilot was then assigned a target, and they would make a head-on approach at an altitude some 915 metres above the bombers so as to avoid contact with any enemy fighter escorts.

A coloured stripe was painted on the nose of each aircraft attached to the *Kommando*, and this slanted downward toward the front of the jet at an angle of 16 degrees below the horizontal. Upon reaching the correct distance from the target (calculated to be about 2740 metres), the pilot would commence his attack dive, using the stripe to line up the formation. The four-degree differential between the 20-degree attack angle and the 16-degree stripe was compensated by the time it took to go into the dive at a speed of 750-800 km/h.

At a distance of 550 metres, the bombs would be released – each weapon was fitted with a Type 89B 2 second-delay fuse. Trials were also conducted with the *Baro 1* barometric fuse (which was hampered by the cold air flow around the aircraft), the acoustic *Ameise* fuse (which, due to its sensitivity, was susceptible to damage during transport) and an electrical remote-controlled type known as the *Pollux*, designed by Blaupunkt. The latter was to be used in conjunction with the FuG 16.

Having released their bombs, the Me 262s would then break away by 'split-essing' or climbing over the bombers and returning to base.

Various weapons arrangements were tested by the *Kommando* over the Müritz See – often using an Me 262 flown by Berliner Hanns Gross – to establish blast radius, dispersal during fall and fuse performance. Little data was gathered from these experiments though, as the bombs often failed to explode. As a result of these problems, it was never ascertained which was the most effective and practical arrangement. Ordnance types included the AB 500 container loaded with either 25 SD 15 Zt semi armour-piercing bombs equipped with time fuses or 84 SD 3s. Another variation was to fill the AB 500 with 4000 *Brandtaschen* incendiary pellets and enough explosives to scatter them with sufficient velocity – similar to that of a massive shotgun blast – to penetrate the skin of a heavy bomber.

However, during testing it was found that after the canister had opened, the bombs hit each other and detonated too quickly, with the resultant

The AB 500 weapons container, loaded with semi armour-piercing bombs or incendiaries, was amongst the ordnance trialled by *Kommando Stamp* during its air-to-air bombing experiments with the Me 262

blast severely damaging the carrier aircraft. On one such occasion, the bombs detonated prematurely and Hanns Gross had to make a forced-landing in a meadow. Badly wounded, he was subsequently hospitalised for several weeks.

Individual SC 250 (with a time fuse), SC 500, SD 250 and SD 500 bombs were also tested. Ultimately, however, it was decided to use the AB 500 filled with 370 kg of Triolin explosive in any eventual operations. To provide some degree of accuracy, in January 1945 Dr Kortmann (a physicist at the Zeiss works in Jena) designed the *Gegner-Pfeil-Visier* 1 (GPV 1) reflex bombsight, of which some 20 units were manufactured.

Herbert Schlüter recalled;

'What was innovative about our bombs was the barometric fuse. It consisted of a box that contained a barometer connected by a tube to the static outside pressure. The opening and closing of this tube could be operated with a button from the cockpit. The bomb consisted of a container made of sheet metal designed like a bomb, with stabilisers as used by the Luftwaffe. The casing contained two identical bowl-shaped containers that were connected to the altitude stabiliser by means of a hinge pin. In front, both containers were closed. This container was used to spread small bomblets, whereby the closed-off portion of the container was detonated by an adjustable fuse.

Previously assigned to Kommando Nowotny, this aircraft was photographed in late 1944 whilst being used by Kommando Stamp in bomb-dropping trials. The jet has been fitted with a specially faired 'Wikingerschiff' ('Viking Ship') ordnance rack that has two 500-kg SC 500 bombs affixed to it. The latter weapons were also tested by Kommando Stamp for possible employment in the air-to-air bombing role

'For the barometric bomb, only the casing was needed. A tube filled with explosives that was almost as long as the bomblet container was installed in the middle of the casing. Some 4000 "incendiary packets" were then placed around the tube. The packets contained round pieces of magnesium that had been drilled open and filled with thermite, which is a mixture of aluminium oxide and pulverised iron. It is used to weld steel railway tracks. Thermite and magnesium burn at a temperature of 2000 degrees centigrade.'

Values for the relative speeds of the Me 262 and the bomber formation, the relative altitude from which the bombs were to be dropped and the necessary ballistics figures for the type of bomb being used were adjusted in the reflex sight before take-off. Although, as has been stated, the dive angle was set at 20 degrees, a lever to allow last minute manual override was installed in the left side of the cockpit. The pilot would then simply move the lever until its long axis was parallel to the horizontal plane in which the bomber formation was flying. He would then wait until the wing tips of a B-17 were framed by his reflex bombsight (this occurred at a distance of 550 metres), at which point the bombs were released.

The pilots of Stamp's *Kommando* prepared for their task using a specially equipped Me 262 cockpit section assembled by Zeiss at Jena, into which had been fitted a GPV 1. A film projector then threw an image of an approaching bomber formation onto a white wall, so that it appeared as if the cockpit were 'approaching' a target. Herbert Schlüter remembers the illusion as being perfect;

'Zeiss had developed the new ram bombsight and we were to train with it. We met the men responsible for its development. There was Dr Kortmann and Dr Schneider, who was a mathematician, and a few others who explained the workings of the new sight.

'The training took place in an improvised cockpit fitted with a ram bombsight. Ten metres in front of the mock-up was a big screen. An original image of a frontal view of an American bomber formation was projected onto the screen – it was very realistic. At first the formation was small, being just a dot, but it rapidly became larger in front of our eyes.

'The Me 262 in a five- or seven-degree dive could quickly reach 940-960 km/h. The bombers flew at around 400 km/h. The simulator made it very clear to us that the closing speed was 1350 km/h. We trained from morning till night with few breaks in between. After every "attack", our co-workers from Zeiss told us how many "hits" we had.'

It took, on average, about five days for a pilot to become proficient at using the GPV 1.

The *Kommando* returned to Lärz from Jena after about a week. As Herbert Schlüter recalled;

'Finally, the day arrived. The *Kommandeur* had picked me to test the first bomb over Lake Müritz. I was to drop the bomb from an altitude of 8000 metres in the same manner as we had practised at Jena, but without the ram sight. I pushed the button to close the capillary tube between the barometric device and the static outside air pressure and climbed to 8000 metres. After a short dive, I dropped the bomb and went into a turn to observe the fireball. Nothing happened – the bomb did not explode. This was a big disappointment for all concerned. Dr Schneider – the "human calculator" – from Zeiss called his firm and told them about the failure.

'Another try was planned for the next day. The barometric fuse was carefully examined, but another failure was the order of the day. Another try had the same negative result. Then the fuses were tested with training bombs over the target area. Despite an intensive search, the problem could not be determined, so we looked for alternative possibilities. We tried detonating the bombs without the use of a barometric fuse.

'Only much later was the cause of the problem found. The capillary consisted of a very thin rubber hose that could be closed by means of a solenoid and a push button from the cockpit. The rubber hose became permeable or porous in the cold and the fuse failed as a result. It would have been quite simple to have tested the device under operational conditions, as a small chamber equipped with a vacuum pump, an altimeter, some dry ice, a thermometer and a few aircraft instruments would have done the trick. The inventors of the barometric fuse – two professors from the university of Braunschweig and Brünn – were just too theoretical.'

Engineers arrived from Blaupunkt to work on the radio-controlled *Pollux* fuses. Herbert Schlüter remembered;

'The next series of experiments was conducted with radio-controlled fuses. Two engineers from the electronics firm Blaupunkt joined us and proceeded to install their devices into our aircraft and our bombs. Many bombs were then dropped over the test site, but the results were not good. Radio-controlled fuses proved to be unreliable and were discontinued.

'Other tests were conducted with small fragmentation bombs that were dropped in large containers. The containers were blown open by means of a pre-set timing fuse and the small fragmentation bombs scattered like shotgun blast. At first, the experiments were conducted with 2-kg SD 2 bombs. The problem was that these weapons, used in conjunction with the ram sight and the large container, did not become live quick enough. The tail of the SD 2 bomb had a small propeller in the rear that began to rotate when dropped, and after a number of rotations it armed the bomb. In order to shorten this time, we manipulated the mechanical fuse. This was dangerous work, especially when carried out by amateurs. These experiments proved fruitless as well.

'We tried even small fragmentation bombs. One bomb had a streamlined designed and weighed about 2 kg. There was a tiny propeller up front on a short 2 cm tube, into which were drilled several holes. The air passing through the holes determined the rotation of the propeller. After a certain number of rotations, the bomb was armed. But it still took too long to arm the weapon to make the system effective. So, in order to arm the bomb more rapidly, more holes were drilled into the tube – this was a mistake, as we were soon to find out!

'A 250-kg bomb container was packed with SD 2s in preparation for a test flight over the target by a staff engineer from the *Erprobungsstelle* Rechlin. Gerd Stamp and his five pilots went to Rechlin to observe the tests. The Me 262 approached at a height of only 400-500 metres. The bomb container was dropped directly in front of us, and we watched as it "flew" just a few metres below and behind the aircraft.

'After a short time, the container opened and the small bombs dropped out like a shotgun blast. Then something happened which took our breath away. We saw that two of the bombs touched each other and exploded, which then set off a chain reaction of explosions. The result was a tremendous fireball just a short distance behind the aircraft – maybe 100 metres. We could also see that the aircraft must have been damaged, because it rapidly lost altitude before disappearing behind some trees. The pilot was lucky, since his jet was still under partial control, and he crash-landed at about 400 km/h. He was badly injured, but it could have been worse.

'We also tried out heavier bombs. The first time I dropped such a weapon, I made a surprising observation. Hanns Gross and I had the task of each dropping a time-fused 250-kg bomb from 4000 metres above Lake Müritz. We flew 40 metres apart and had sight and radio contact. We were flying at high speed when I gave the order to drop the bombs. I felt a jolt as the bomb was released, and at the same time saw Hanns' bomb drop. To my surprise, the bomb did not fall "direction Earth", but only down about three metres. It stayed in a horizontal position beneath the aircraft and continued along with the same velocity. I observed this for a few seconds. The timing device was running, and we decided to peel away rapidly from the danger zone! Eyewitnesses on the ground later told us "our performance was impressive!"'

Trials continued throughout January 1945, but little practical success was achieved, and the few experiments that were conducted were plagued with problems. The runway at Lärz was only partially constructed of concrete, and during an unexpected thaw in the winter weather, the unit experienced great difficulty in just getting an aircraft airborne. One attempt was broken off on account of insufficient air speed being reached, whilst on another, the jet became coated with mud and had to be hosed down by local firefighters. Herbert Schlüter recalled;

'It was at the end of February 1945 that the *Kommandeur* ordered Eberhard Gzik and I to fly to Erfurt-Bindersleben to get ram sights installed into our aircraft. The work was to be done by technicians from Zeiss at Jena. We flew there without encountering any problems. It was a cold winter, and the ground was covered with snow and ice. The work on our jets – both to the cockpit and rear fuselage – took a week to complete.

'The weather changed during our time at Erfurt-Bindersleben, with the temperature rising above zero and the snowfall changing to rain. The work was completed and I was the first to take off. I lined up my aircraft, stepped on the brakes and slowly pushed the throttles forward until the brakes would not hold the jet anymore. Then I released the brakes and accelerated to full power. The aircraft accelerated quickly, but as soon as I began to leave the area of concrete surface, the landing gear started to sink into the softer ground and I slowed down considerably. Despite giving full power, the aircraft never exceeded 140 km/h – not sufficient to get airborne. It would have taken at least 200 km/h, and so I aborted take-off.'

Undeterred, the *Kommando Stamp* pilots waited three days for a pair of 1000 kp Rheinmetall-Borsig rocket-assisted take-off units to arrive to fit to one of the Me 262s. Unfortunately, the units came with no installation and operating instructions, so two local electricians were called upon to do the job. Finally, the aircraft was made ready and, despite "miserable weather", a large crowd gathered to watch Herbert Schlüter make the rocket-assisted take-off at the beginning of a short transfer flight to

Weimar, where a Zeiss sight was due to be installed. After initial pre-flight checks, the Me 262 – its fuel tanks only half full – rushed up into a "milky sky" of almost ten-tenths cloud, with visibility down to 300 metres.

Dropping the burnt-out rocket units over the field, Schlüter made a turn, only to discover that his compass was malfunctioning. No longer able to locate Lärz, and failing in his attempts to make radio contact with other nearby airfields, he climbed above the cloud and, keeping the sun behind him, headed north away from Allied occupied territory.

Eventually, Schlüter managed to make contact with the airfield at Sachau, near Gardelegen. At 7000 metres, he began his descent through the cloud, although his attempts at orientation without a compass proved fruitless. Using the bank and turn indicator, he broke through the ceiling at 200 metres into driving rain, with little daylight – despite the fact that it was midday. Passing over what he took to be the main Hannover-Berlin railway line, he approached the nearby *Autobahn* and briefly considered making an emergency landing. Discounting this option, Schlüter pushed on to the nearest airfield at Braunschweig-Waggum. On his last drop of fuel he landed on his second approach.

Lack of J2 fuel at Braunschweig almost prevented his attempt to reach Weimar the next day. However, the airfield staff concocted a mixture of B4 fuel and motor oil, and with improved weather, Schlüter flew to Weimar without difficulty. When he landed he was advised that *Kommando Stamp* had been transferred to Brandenburg-Briest!

In a report dated 3 February, Generalmajor Eckhard Christian, the Chief of the Luftwaffe's Operations Staff, recommended to von Brauchitsch that *Kommando Stamp* be disbanded 'at once'.

'The essential objections', Christian wrote, 'are that the enemy will again immediately prevent bomb-dropping by using fighter escort at an even higher altitude, in addition to the normal escort. By exploiting the necessarily long bombing run, enemy fighters using a 1,000-metre height advantage have a clear chance of shooting down even jet aircraft. The present type of enemy formation offers the least favourable conditions for breaking up a formation. By and large, the results of Major Stamp's experiment are still wide open. The procedures are still uncertain, and have not been tested tactically. These considerations lead to the belief that, in spite of the improved technical position, no lasting success is to be expected.

'In the present situation, the necessary tests, personnel adjustments, material expenditure etc., do not appear justified. In order to carry out the *Führer's* demands, the immediate need is to assemble all Me 262s for operation as quickly as possible. Six Me 262s were assigned to *Kommando Stamp* and four have been allocated. It does not appear justifiable to divert aircraft of this type for an experiment which will not produce conclusive results in a short time period. The *Luftwaffenführungsstab* proposes that Major Stamp's project is dropped at once.'

The *Reichsmarschall's* office gave its backing to Christian's report the same day, and on 7 February the OKL Daily Situation Report noted;

'Major Stamp has worked out a new plan for air-to-air bombing against heavy bomber formations, and is at present testing its practical possibilities. He has already been allocated four Me 262s for this purpose, and another two have been earmarked. In a detailed criticism of the

A line-up of Me 262s believed to have been photographed just prior to their delivery to JG 7, with civilian weapons and ballistics technicians supervising the installation of WGr 21 mortar tubes. Note the unusual diagonally striped camouflage on the Me 262 in the centre foreground

In early February 1945, Göring supported a proposal from the Chief of the Luftwaffe's Operations Staff that *Kommando Stamp* be disbanded and its personnel and equipment integrated into a JG 7 *Stabsstaffel*. Under this new designation, the elements of the former *Kommando* carried out trials using the 21 cm WGr 21 air-to-air mortar and, later, 55 mm R4M rockets. Here, two Me 262A-1as of JG 7, seen at either Brandenburg-Briest or Parchim, are fitted with mortar tubes. The machine in the foreground, 'Green 1', carries a distinctive diagonally striped camouflage scheme, with markings thought to have been those of the *Kommandeur* of III./JG 7, Major Rudolf Sinner

prospects of success, which will be very slight in the foreseeable future, the Chief of the Operations Staff suggests to the *Reichsmarschall* that the Stamp Detachment be disbanded immediately, or attached to JG 7 if the tests are to be continued.'

Shortly thereafter, *Kommando Stamp's* aircraft and personnel were indeed integrated into JG 7, becoming known as *Stabsstaffel* JG 7. Still employed in the test and development roles, the *Stamp* pilots cleared the Me 262 to use 21 cm WGr 21 air-to-air mortars and 55 mm R4M rockets against Allied bombers.

The first of these weapons to be fitted to the jet fighter was the WGr 21 mortar. Designed as an infantry weapon for use in ground warfare, the original concept was to install the spin-stabilised mortars under the wings of Fw 190s for use against four-engined bombers, where the blast effect from a shell exploding within the confines of a formation would scatter

the *Viermots*, thus weakening their defensive firepower and rendering individual bombers more vulnerable to attack.

The weapon was used in numbers for the first time on 28 July 1943 during an American raid on Kassel and Oschersleben, and results were acceptable in as much as blast fragmentation from them did break up the bombers and a number were claimed destroyed as an indirect result. Mortars were subsequently fitted to Bf 109G-6s of IV./JG 3, I., II. and III./JG 53, I. and III./JG 77 and I./JG 5, and they were used to varying effect in the Mediterranean and Rumania from August 1943 until early 1944. Other similarly-equipped Bf 109s of 7./JG 3, 5./JG 11, 2./JG 27 and 6./JG 51 operated in the defence of the Reich, and a number of Bf 110G-2/R-3 *Zerstörer* of ZG 76 and Me 410As of ZG 26 carried pairs of twin mortar sets, in addition to an array of cannon and machine guns, when used as heavily-armed bomber-destroyers.

Although further trials continued through until mid-1944 with the aim of improving the WGr 21, it was soon found that the weapon's main shortcoming was its lack of velocity (a maximum of 320 m/sec). This in turn made it extremely difficult to aim, and it usually exploded harmlessly either short of the target or past it. The launch tubes also robbed German fighters – particularly the heavier *Zerstörer* – of their performance, making them vulnerable to Allied fighters.

Senior Luftwaffe fighter commanders recognised the psychological effect the mortars had on bomber crews, but also noted that when the tubes were fitted to the Fw 190, the fighter lost some 40-50 km/h from its top speed and also suffered restrictions in its ceiling and manoeuvrability. The German fighters also lacked a range-measuring device, and therefore pilots had no way of controlling the point of detonation.

As a makeshift measure, two of these weapons were mounted on bomb racks beneath the fuselage of an Me 262 and tested operationally by the *Stabsstaffel* of JG 7, but for how long, and what the effects were, is not known.

Luftwaffe photographic records for 1944-45 suggest that JG 7 was not afraid to experiment with camouflage schemes on its jet fighters – a sensible endeavour, given the increasing threat posed by Allied fighter-bombers operating at will over the unit's bases. Here, Me 262A-1a 'Green 3' of the *Geschwaderstab* prepares to move off across the concrete surface at Brandenburg-Briest in February or early March 1945. The aircraft is finished in a relatively rare application of streaked horizontal lines, and has been fitted with a pair of 21 cm WGr 21 air-to-air mortar tubes beneath the fuselage aft of the nosewheel

COLOUR PLATES

1
Me 262A-1a 'White 7' of Oberfeldwebel Hermann
Buchner, *Kommando Nowotny*, Lechfeld, October 1944

2
Me 262A-1a 'Green 1' of Major Rudolf Sinner,
Stab III./JG 7, Brandenburg-Briest, January 1945

3
Me 262A-1a 'Green 1' of Major Rudolf Sinner,
Stab III./JG 7, Brandenburg-Briest, January 1945

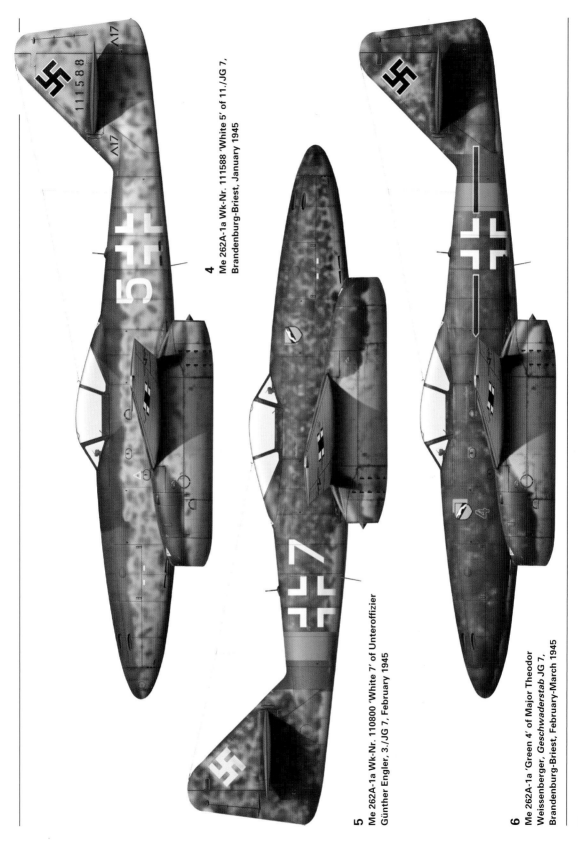

4

Me 262A-1a Wk-Nr. 111588 'White 5' of 11./JG 7, Brandenburg-Briest, January 1945

5

Me 262A-1a Wk-Nr. 110800 'White 7' of Unteroffizier Günther Engler, 3./JG 7, February 1945

6

Me 262A-1a 'Green 4' of Major Theodor Weissenberger, *Geschwaderstab* JG 7, Brandenburg-Briest, February-March 1945

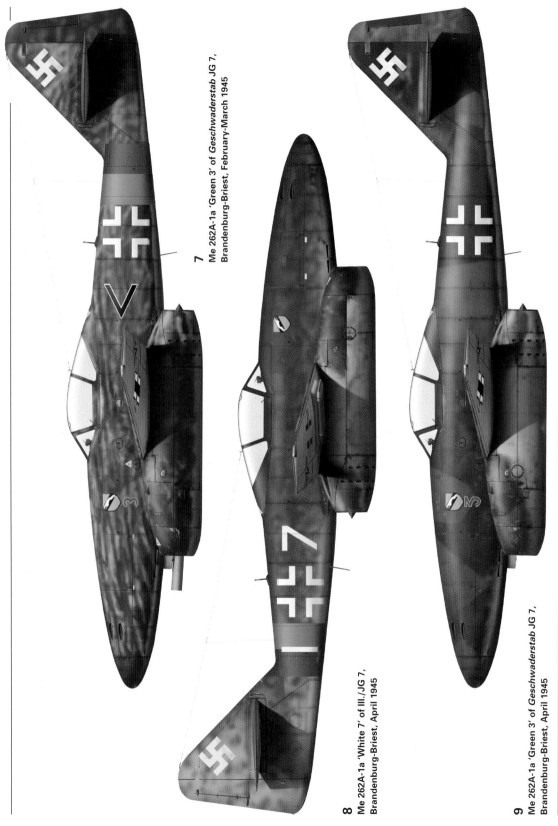

7
Me 262A-1a 'Green 3' of *Geschwaderstab* JG 7,
Brandenburg-Briest, February-March 1945

8
Me 262A-1a 'White 7' of III./JG 7,
Brandenburg-Briest, April 1945

9
Me 262A-1a 'Green 3' of *Geschwaderstab* JG 7,
Brandenburg-Briest, April 1945

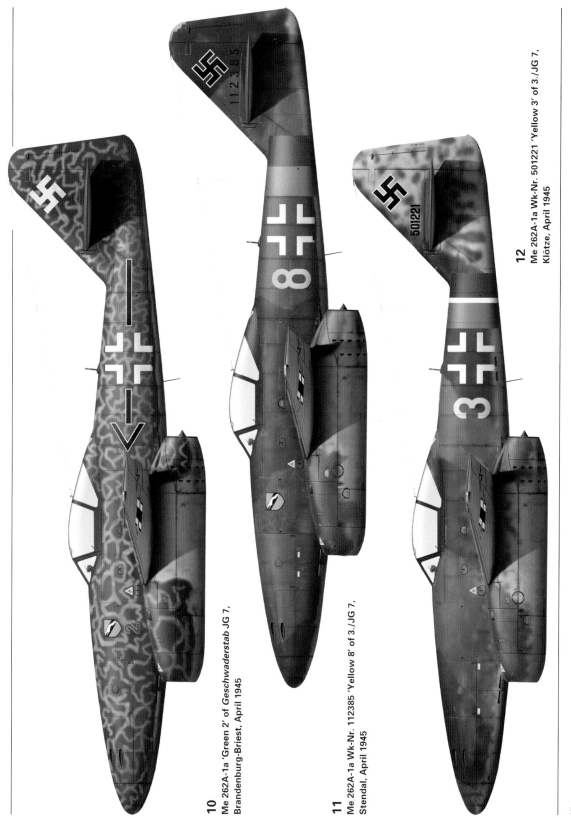

10
Me 262A-1a 'Green 2' of *Geschwaderstab* JG 7,
Brandenburg-Briest, April 1945

11
Me 262A-1a Wk-Nr. 112385 'Yellow 8' of 3./JG 7,
Stendal, April 1945

12
Me 262A-1a Wk-Nr. 501221 'Yellow 3' of 3./JG 7,
Klötze, April 1945

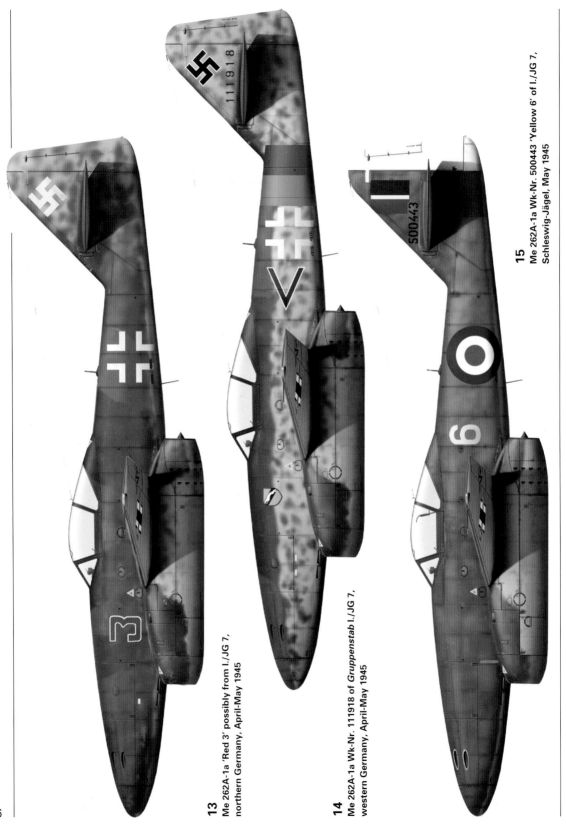

13
Me 262A-1a 'Red 3' possibly from I./JG 7,
northern Germany, April-May 1945

14
Me 262A-1a Wk-Nr. 111918 of *Gruppenstab* I./JG 7,
western Germany, April-May 1945

15
Me 262A-1a Wk-Nr. 500443 'Yellow 6' of I./JG 7,
Schleswig-Jägel, May 1945

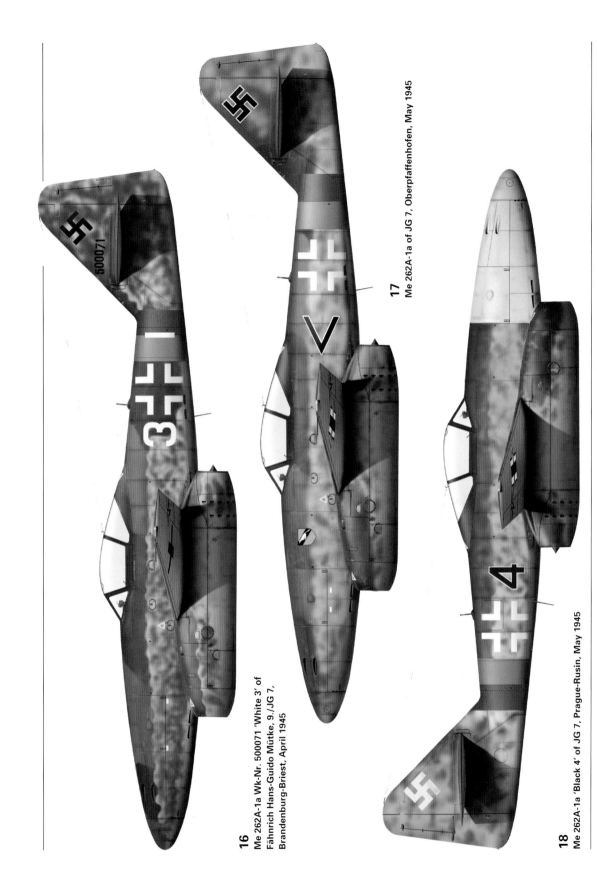

16
Me 262A-1a Wk-Nr. 500071 'White 3' of Fähnrich Hans-Guido Mütke, 9./JG 7, Brandenburg-Briest, April 1945

17
Me 262A-1a of JG 7, Oberpfaffenhofen, May 1945

18
Me 262A-1a 'Black 4' of JG 7, Prague-Rusin, May 1945

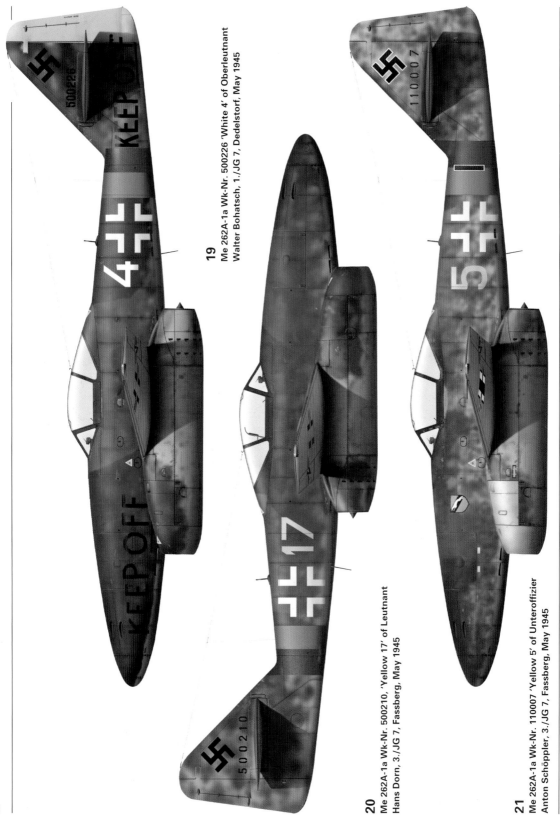

19
Me 262A-1a Wk-Nr. 500226 'White 4' of Oberleutnant
Walter Bohatsch, 1./JG 7, Dedelstorf, May 1945

20
Me 262A-1a Wk-Nr. 500210, 'Yellow 17' of Leutnant
Hans Dorn, 3./JG 7, Fassberg, May 1945

21
Me 262A-1a Wk-Nr. 110007 'Yellow 5' of Unteroffizier
Anton Schöppler, 3./JG 7, Fassberg, May 1945

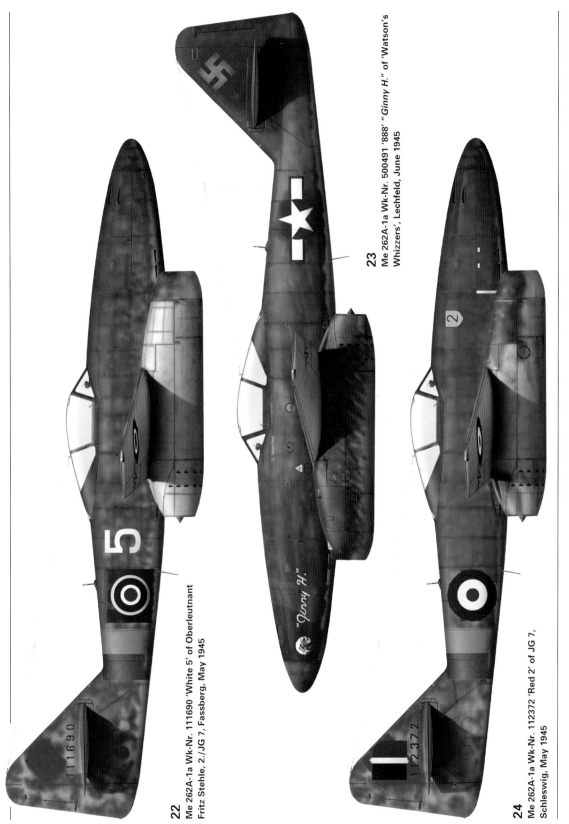

22
Me 262A-1a Wk-Nr. 111690 'White 5' of Oberleutnant
Fritz Stehle, 2./JG 7, Fassberg, May 1945

23
Me 262A-1a Wk-Nr. 500491 '888' *"Ginny H."* of 'Watson's
Whizzers', Lechfeld, June 1945

24
Me 262A-1a Wk-Nr. 112372 'Red 2' of JG 7,
Schleswig, May 1945

1
Rare white version of JG 7 emblem
seen on *Kommodore's* jet

2
Non-standard cross-legged version
of JG 7's running fox emblem

3
Standard JG 7 running fox emblem,
applied to port side of jet

4
Standard running fox emblem on
darker blue background

5
Standard JG 7 running fox emblem,
applied to starboard side of jet

6
Partially completed JG 7 running fox
emblem, as seen on at least one jet

ATTRITION

The beginning of March 1945 saw the *Gruppen* of JG 7 dispersed as follows; I./JG 7 was at Brandenburg-Briest under Major Erich Rudorffer, with 1./JG 7 at Kaltenkirchen under Oberleutnant Hans Grünberg, 2./JG 7 at Kaltenkirchen under Oberleutnant Fritz Stehle and 3./JG 7 at Oranienburg under Oberleutnant Hans-Peter Waldmann. II./JG 7 was at Neumünster under Hauptmann Lutz-Wilhelm Burckhardt, with 5., 6., and 7./JG 7 all at Neumünster. And III./JG 7 was at Brandenburg-Briest under Major Rudolf Sinner, with 9./JG 7 at Brandenburg-Briest under Oberleutnant Joachim Weber, 10./JG 7 at Oranienburg under Oberleutnant Franz Schall and 11./JG 7 at Parchim under Oberleutnant Günther Wegmann.

After a three-day lull following the American raid of 28 February, JG 7 was back in action on 3 March, when the *Geschwader Stab* and III./JG 7 combined to send up 29 Me 262s from all three III. *Gruppe* airfields against a USAAF raid of more than 1000 heavy bombers targeting oil, armaments and transport targets across northern and central Germany. The 'heavies' were escorted by nearly 700 fighters.

At 1015 hrs, the jets attacked the B-17s of the 3rd Air Division in line astern from 6000-7000 metres between Braunschweig and Magdeburg. Hauptmann Heinz Gutmann (a former bomber pilot with III./KG 53 and a Knight's Cross holder now flying with 10./JG 7), the veteran *Kdo. Nowotny* pilot Leutnant Karl Schnörrer of 11./JG 7 and Oberfeldwebel Helmut Lennartz of 9./JG 7 each claimed a B-17 destroyed, while Oberfähnrich Heinz Russel of 9./JG 7 and Oberfeldwebel Hermann Buchner managed to shoot down a P-47 and P-51, respectively, with Buchner also claiming a B-17. He recalled;

'We broke through the fighter escorts, but then found ourselves under massive defensive fire from the bombers' turret gunners. When we were about 1000 metres from the bombers, Gutmann's cockpit flashed with fire and his fighter sheared away from our formation and dived away vertically. I think he might have been killed outright, as he did not attempt to bale out.'

Gutmann's Me 262 hit the ground a few kilometres south of Braunschweig.

For his part, Russel, another former *Kdo. Nowotny* pilot, had actually targeted a B-17, but just as he opened fire with his 30 mm MK 108 cannon, a P-47 flew across his path and was blown apart in mid-air.

Over Magdeburg, Me 262s from 10. and 11./JG 7 took on more B-17s, as well as the 219 B-24s of the 2nd Air Division sent to bomb the oil refinery at Rothensee. Oberfeldwebel Heinz Arnold shot down a B-17 and a P-47, while *Gruppenkommandeur* Major Rudi Sinner claimed a B-24. Initially, his *Schwarm* had made a frontal attack against the Liberators, but without success, so he decided – despite the challenge of passing through the formation without collision – to go in accompanied only by his wingman, Leutnant Müller, from the rear. As Sinner did so, all four of his MK 108s jammed just after he had opened fire on a selected

Hauptmann Heinz Gutmann had flown He 111s with I. and III./KG 53 prior to transferring to 10./JG 7 in early 1945. He had been awarded the Knight's Cross on 5 April 1944 while an oberleutnant with 3./KG 53. His Me 262 was hit by the defensive fire from a bomber formation on 3 March 1945 and he was killed

Groundcrew clad in their ubiquitous black overalls attend to the 30 mm MK 108 cannon in the nose of JG 7's 'White 8' in readiness for another mission from Brandenburg-Briest in early 1945. The figure standing on the wing might actually be the pilot of the aircraft

Clad in typical late-war flying garb, the pilots of 11./JG 7 line up for a *Staffel* photograph probably at Parchim some time in March 1945. They are, from left to right Oberfeldwebel Heinz Arnold, Unteroffizier Heiner Geisthövel, Feldwebel Franz Köster, Unteroffizier Hellmut Detjens, Leutnant Joachim Weber, Unteroffizier Ernst Giefing, Feldwebel Wilhelm Bergmann, Feldwebel Heinz Eichner, Oberfeldwebel August Lübking and Leutnant Fritz Müller. Attrition took its toll, as Weber, Eichner and Lübking were all killed in action during 21-22 March, Geisthövel was lost on the 30th and Arnold was killed on 17 April

B-24, so he broke away. Sinner had, however, noticed a brief flash on the bomber's wing. The following day, a local flak unit reported the downing of a B-24 in the same location that the combat had taken place, so Sinner was credited with the victory.

In their post-mission report, USAAF Intelligence Officers recorded;

'Analysis of Me 262 tactics on 3 March reveals that the jets preferred to attack from either "six" or "twelve o'clock". In most cases, attacks from other directions turned out to be feints. No preference was shown regarding the level of approach, but high approaches were generally not very high and low ones not very low. The number making a particular pass varied from one to four, but when more than one attacked, an echelon (almost in trail) formation was typically used. Breakaways varied considerably, although they always combined a change in altitude with a change in direction. Bomb groups were bounced while strung out in bombing formation, and the jets completely ignored German flak while attacking.

'The Me 262 pilots did not seem to be particular as to which group in the bomber column they attacked, and they were not averse to climbing back for a second pass after diving away from the first one. In some instances, the jets seemed to glide with power off when attacking, probably to obtain a longer firing burst by lessening the rate of closure.'

Six *Viermots* had fallen to the guns of JG 7 and three escort fighters also became victims. Although the USAAF claimed six Me 262s shot down, such losses are not recorded on the German side.

It seems the intensity of operations subsided a little over the next few days, mainly due to adverse weather, although 1. *Jagddivision* reported five Me 262s on patrol on 7 March – they did not encounter the enemy. Two days later, Heinz Russel (a victor on the 3 March mission over Braunschweig) was killed when his Me 262 was sent up to intercept an F-6 Mustang photographic reconnaissance aircraft over Kiel. Some sources state that he may have collided with the American aircraft west of Vysted, near Leland, since neither aircraft returned.

On 14 March Leutnante Weber and Alfred Ambs (who had joined JG 7 from JG 104) and Unteroffizier Ernst Giefing, all of III. *Gruppe*, took off from Briest to intercept enemy reconnaissance aircraft following an *Alarmstart* order at Briest. After flying for some 20 minutes, the three pilots spotted a pair of Mustangs flying west. Weber opened fire prematurely and, alerted to the Messerschmitts' presence, the P-51s took evasive action. Following a dummy break, the jets used their superior speed to veer round and attack the Americans from head-on. Opening fire from 300 metres, Ambs watched one of the Mustangs explode before him. The next day, 1. *Jagddivision* reported that JG 7 had sent nine Me 262s out on patrol.

Meanwhile, a dramatic new development was underway that would strengthen JG 7's arsenal significantly.

For many months, German ballistics engineers had recognised that the installation of rockets would become 'indispensable' as the possibility of introducing greater ranges of fixed armament into a single fighter aircraft became increasingly difficult. Such an improvement was desperately needed due to Allied bomber formations increasing their defensive firepower.

Throughout the latter half of 1943 and into 1944, following the mixed success of the WGr 21 mortar, German armaments experts recognised that the only plausible alternative was for a fighter formation to attack a bomber *Pulk* simultaneously with batteries of rockets carried either in underwing racks or in nose mounted 'honeycombs'. These weapons would allow a dense 'fire-chain' to be created that would be impossible for the bombers to avoid.

In June 1944, a requirement was put forward by the Luftwaffe's Technical Equipment Office for an electrically fired, fin-stabilised weapon whose warhead would contain sufficient explosive to destroy a four-engined bomber in one hit. Four weeks later, a powerful consortium of companies, each with individual responsibility for different components, was formed and led by the Deutsches Waffen und Munitions Fabrik (DWM) Research Institute of Lübeck.

This consortium duly presented the Technical Equipment Office with a proposal for an 814 mm long, 55 mm calibre rocket with a warhead containing 520 grams of HTA explosive and ignited by an AZR 2 detonator. The total weight for the weapon was just 3500 grams. The rocket was intended to be launched against aerial targets from a range of 800 metres, with in-flight stabilisation being provided by eight fins that were opened automatically by aerodynamic drag immediately after launching.

The proposal was received favourably and the designation 'R4M' *(Rakete 4 kg Minenkopf)* applied to the project. Firing trials took place at the end of October 1944 on the Strehla range at the Westin works of Brünn AG and at Kurt Heber at Osteroda. However, the *Erprobungsstellen* at Rechlin (which had conducted the first air launches in December 1944) and Tarnewitz both judged that the missile was still unsatisfactory as a result of the poor standard of manufacture of some individual parts. By the end of January 1945, once initial burn-out problems had finally been solved, a general re-working of the rocket, incorporating various aerodynamic and warhead refinements, was conducted.

In its final form, the R4M appeared as an unrotated, rail or tube-launched, single venturi, solid fuel propelled, multi-fin stabilised missile. The warhead was housed in an exceptionally thin 1 mm sheet steel case enclosed in two pressed steel sections that were welded together so as to keep the Hexogen high-explosive charge in place. The missile boasted a high charge-weight to case-weight ratio.

R4Ms were to be carried in wooden underwing racks that were attached by four screws and positioned outboard of the Me 262's engines. The connections between the launch rack and the wing surface were faired in to counteract the possibility of air eddies. The standard launch rack – known as the EG-R4M – measured approximately 700 mm in length, with each rocket being fitted with sliding lugs so that it could hang freely from the guide rails.

Prior to loading into the rack, seven of the R4M's eight fins were held in a folded-down position by binding them with spring-steel wire made with spherical or similarly thickened ends. The wire ends were then crossed and the eighth (free) fin pressed down to hold the other seven in place.

The wooden carrying and launch rack, fitted to the underside starboard wing of an Me 262 from JG 7, from which a battery of 12 55 mm R4M rockets would be fired. With each rack weighing just 20 kg, more than one could be carried beneath each wing

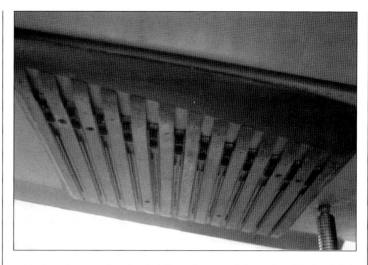

Each rocket was then loaded from the rear of the rack, with the eighth fin held in place by the rail securing the wire binding. The rocket was pushed along the guide-rail until the rear-sliding lug was arrested by a notch in the rail. At the back of each rail was a terminal contact block connecting the ignition wires that hung down close to the socket. Once fired, the eighth fin was designed to spring free, which in turn released the binding wire, thus allowing the remaining seven fins to open – a process that commenced at about 400 mm from the rail and finished once the rocket had flown approximately 2.5 metres.

As many rails as desired could be fitted together to make one launch rack by means of transverse connection, with a gap of 65 mm between each rail, although it was usual to carry a maximum load of 12 R4Ms under each wing of the Me 262 using a 21-kg rack. It was calculated that the loss of speed incurred by an Me 262 as a result of a Heber launch rack being fitted was approximately 16 km/h.

Operational evaluation of the R4M was conducted by Major Georg Christl's *Jagdgruppe* 10, based at Redlin, near Osteroda. Christl's unit had been assigned the task of testing various types of experimental weapons systems produced by manufacturers that were intended specifically as advanced fighter armament in the war against the bombers.

On 21 February 1945, a total of 200 practice missiles (R4M-Gb) was delivered to the unit, but still defects were observed, including corrosion in the combustion chambers and the warheads which DWM diagnosed as a 'non-homogeneous mixing of powder'. These problems were eventually rectified, and a pyrotechnic trials session followed in which the rockets 'smoked around in wild curves', having been fired from a static Fw 190. Christl and his technical officer, Hauptmann Karl Kiefer, then hastily developed a wooden underwing launch rack that was capable of carrying 12 rockets.

Still the pattern of fire dispersal was far too wide, so Christl and Kiefer attempted to launch the missiles at intervals using a bomb release switch taken from a He 177. Eventually it was found that control could be gained if six rockets were fired in two salvoes. Christl recommended that the first consignment of R4Ms be despatched to 11./JG 7's base at Parchim following eventual trouble-free launching on 15 March 1945.

A battery of 12 R4M rockets have been slid into position on the underwing launch rack of this jet from JG 7. Prior to each rocket being loaded into the rack, seven of its eight fins would have been held in a folded-down position by binding them with spring-steel wire made with spherical or similarly thickened ends. The wire ends were then crossed and the eighth fin pressed down to hold the other seven in place. Each rocket would be loaded from the rear of the rack, with the eighth fin held in place by the rail securing the wire binding. The rocket was pushed along the guide rail until the rear sliding lug was arrested by a notch in the rail.

Under the supervision of Willi Langhammer of Messerschmitt Augsburg, twin launch racks, each capable of carrying 12 R4Ms, were fitted to Leutnant Schnörrer's Me 262, which was then immediately flown by Messerschmitt test pilot Fritz Wendel on the request of III./JG 7's *Kommandeur*, Rudolf Sinner. Schnörrer also made two subsequent flights in the aircraft before the weapon mountings were pronounced acceptable. Wendel reported;

'Without further ado, I tested the converted machine. No adverse changes in flying qualities were discovered, except for perhaps a minor loss of air speed in the climb. On 8 March, Leutnant Schnörrer carried out the first firing test. This did not go quite as planned as several rockets failed to leave their rails or burned out on the rack, fortunately without exploding. A second attempt by Schnörrer went so smoothly that his 9. *Staffel* immediately began to convert the other aircraft, and steps were taken to modifiy the *Staffel's* remaining aircraft, as well as those of I. *Gruppe*.'

Two days later the Inspector of Day Fighters, Oberstleutnant Walter Dahl, visited Parchim and watched Oberleutnant Wegmann fly a demonstration in one of the newly armed Me 262s. Using an old Savoia transport aircraft parked on the edge of the airfield as a target, Wegmann made a gentle descent and fired all his rockets. The Savoia was destroyed.

On 16 March Major Weissenberger was flying one of five jets operating against enemy fighter-bombers in the airspace of 1. *Jagddivision* when he shot down a P-51 northwest of Eberswalde during the early afternoon for his first victory in the Me 262. His victory was one of two claimed by the *Geschwader*.

Adverse weather conditions hampered operations and prevented a show of force on the 17th, but JG 7 did manage to send up a small number of Me 262s to intercept USAAF bombers striking at synthetic oil plants at

Ruhland and Böhlen. It was probably against the Ruhland force that Oberleutnant Wegmann and Oberfeldwebel Hubert Göbel, formerly of 3./JG 302, each claimed a B-17 from the groups belonging to the 3rd Air Division, while Unteroffizier Koster was credited with two destroyed. Yet, according to the recollections of Hermann Buchner, the mission was conducted amidst some sourness;

'On account of an operation, Oberleutnant Wegmann was giving a talk. We, the pilots, wanted to fly, but Wegmann was of the opinion that the weather was too bad. The discussion was very lively, and he was simply not prepared to take a note of our argument. After a repeated discussion with only the two of us present, I asked to be transferred to 10. *Staffel*. Wegmann declared that he would think about it.

'During the next mission, I found myself assigned as Number 2 to Wegmann, but I declined the assignment as his *Rottenflieger*. As a result of this Wegmann took away my "Black 11" and flew the operation on the 18th in this machine. He and his *Rottenflieger* were shot down by Mustangs on this mission, and although Wegmann took to his parachute, his *Rottenflieger* was killed. The problem had sorted itself out, and my transfer to 10. *Staffel* subsequently took place.'

18 March had seen nearly 1200 US heavy bombers target railway and armaments factories in the Berlin area. They were escorted by 426 fighters. 9./JG 7 put up six aircraft, each fitted with two underwing batteries of 12 new R4M rockets. The jets intercepted the *Viermots* over Rathenow, and 144 rockets was fired into the American formation from distances of between 400-600 metres. Pilots reported astonishing amounts of debris and aluminium fragments – pieces of wing, engines and cockpits flying through the air from aircraft hit by the missiles.

This Me 262 from 9./JG 7 also boasts a launch rack fully loaded with R4M rockets on the underside of its starboard wing. The *Geschwader's* running fox emblem of JG 7 has been applied in the usual position on the aircraft's nose

Oberfähnrich Walter Windisch, who had joined the Luftwaffe in 1943 and who had two victories to his credit by the time he joined JG 7 from JG 52, was one of the first pilots in the *Geschwader* to experience the effect of the R4M in operational conditions;

'Flying the Me 262 was like a kind of "life insurance". But I was on that first sortie on 18 March during which the R4M rockets were used, and I experienced something beyond my conception. The destructive effect against the targets was immense. It almost gave me a feeling of being invincible. However, the launching grids for the rockets were not of optimum design – they were still too rough and ready. Compared with conventionally powered aircraft, when you went into a turn with the Me 262 flying became a lot more difficult because the trimming was not too good – the grids made this problem even worse.'

Windisch would go on to claim five four-engined bombers shot down while with JG 7, with the first of these falling on 15 March when he accounted for a B-24 of the 2nd Air Division that had been sent to bomb the German military headquarters complex at Zossen.

Leutnant Erich Müller claimed two bombers on 18 March, and a third was credited to Oberfähnrich Pfeiffer.

On the down side, Oberleutnant Günther Wegmann was shot down by return fire from a B-17 that he attacked over the Glöwen area. Severely wounded in the right leg, he attempted to land his badly damaged jet back at Parchim, but its right engine began to burn and he decided to bale out near Wittenberge. Wegmann's leg was eventually amputated. Also lost in this mission as a result of defensive fire from the bombers was Oberleutnant Karl-Heinz Seeler, who had joined JG 7 from 5./JG 302, with whom he had scored seven kills – all four-engined bombers, including four at night.

From Kaltenkirchen, Oberleutnant Grünberg, *Staffelkapitän* of 1./JG 7, reluctantly led a *Schwarm* of Me 262s up against the bombers. Behind him came another three machines let by Oberleutnant Stehle, with a third *Schwarm* led by Oberleutnant Waldmann, commander of 3./JG 7. Grünberg was reluctant because of the weather, and he had expressed his concerns to the fighter control officers of the 2. *Jagddivision* at Stade that the cloudbase was way below the minimum at which it was considered by the *Geschwaderkommodore* to be safe for relatively untrained pilots to take off.

A little later, however, Stade returned Grünberg's call, informing him that no less than *Reichsmarschall* Göring had intervened, brushing aside the pilot's fears and ordering them into the air at the risk of receiving the *Reichsmarshall's* personal 'boot'.

The result was chaos. As Grünberg's *Schwarm* climbed through the cloud to a height of 1000 metres and began to circle, Stehle's echelon quickly followed. Then Waldmann's *Schwarm* began its take-off in a tight, wing-tip to wing-tip formation and things soon began to go wrong. First, Oberfeldwebel Gerhard Reiher's jet fighter suffered an engine failure and was left languishing on the ground. The three remaining jets climbed, with Leutnant Weihs in the centre, flanked by Waldmann to his left and Oberfähnrich Günther Schrey, who had joined JG 7 from JG 3, to his right. Moments later, according to Weihs, Waldmann disappeared from view into the cloud. Shortly after that, his aircraft collided with Weihs' machine amidst the dense cloud. Weihs recalled, 'I went into a flat spin, scrambled out of the cockpit and onto the wing in order to parachute to the ground'.

Weihs came down by parachute in a field near to a station master's house close to the main Hamburg-Berlin railway line. As he landed, he heard the sound of his aircraft crashing into the ground, followed seconds later by that of Waldmann's. The latter had failed to open his parachute, and his body was later discovered by a *Volkssturm* unit near Schwarzenbek, some distance from his aircraft.

Meanwhile, Oberfähnrich Schrey had broken through the overcast only to cross the path of a formation of P-51 Mustangs, which turned into him and shot him down. Although he managed to bale out, a board of enquiry later concluded that the unfortunate pilot had been fired upon by the enemy fighters while descending in his parachute. His body was found near Eggenbüttel. Both he and Waldmann were buried with military honours at Kaltenkirchen.

I. and III./JG 7 had deployed 37 aircraft against the bombers on 18 March, and 13 of them had engaged the enemy. Two pilots reported probable victories, and there were six *Herausschüsse* – incidents of bombers being 'cut out' and forced away from their formations. The *Geschwader* suffered the loss of three pilots, with another badly wounded, while five jets had to be written off due to severe battle damage, with a further two requiring repair.

Nevertheless, the 18th was the first real indication of what impact a small, determined force of jet fighters could have upon the enemy – even allowing for poor operating conditions. USAAF Intelligence later graphically recorded;

'The jets launched their attacks from out of contrails and aggressively pressed home against the last two groups, in one instance to within 50 yards. Several concentrated attacks were made by two or four jets – others attacked singly. Jets made skilful use of superior speed, and though escort fighters engaged, only one jet was claimed damaged. Some 12-15 Me 262s made strong attacks on 3rd Division from west of Salzwedel to Berlin – attacks, though not continuous, were skilful and aggressive, contrail being used to good effect. Six bombers were lost to this attack.

'Initial attack, 20 minutes before target, was on the low squadron of the second group in the column, which, at the time, was strung out and in poor formation. Four Me 262s in a formation similar to that used by P-51s came out of clouds and contrails from "5 o'clock low", closing from 75 yards to point-blank range – three bombers were badly damaged in this attack. Second attack, by three Me 262s, came in from "6.30" to "7 o'clock", low to level, resulting in the tail section of a B-17 being shot off.'

On 19 March 1. *Jagddivision* reported 33 Me 262s of JG 7 operational against enemy bombers over *'Mitteldeutschland'*. This day, in conditions of thick cloud, a force of 374 B-17s of the 3rd Air Division struck their secondary targets of the Zeiss optical works at Jena and motor vehicle plants at Zwickau and in the city of Plauen.

A force of Me 262s from III./JG 7, believed to have been led by Walter Nowotny's old wingman, Leutnant Schnörrer, who had assumed temporary command of 11. *Staffel* following Wegmann's injury, rose to intercept shortly after 1350 hrs. Four B-17s were quickly clawed out of the sky, the victims of Schnörrer – who recorded his 41st victory north of

Leutnant Friedrich Wilhelm 'Timo' Schenk joined JG 7 from JG 300 and flew his first combat sortie in the Me 262 after just three training flights. Nevertheless, he accounted for a Lancaster shot down on 31 March and a Liberator on 4 April 1945

Chemnitz – Oberleutnant Schall and jet 'veterans' Oberfeldwebel Lennartz and Arnold. A further three bombers were damaged to the extent that that they were forced to leave the shelter of their formations to become 'stragglers', thus becoming easy pickings for the piston-engined fighters on the way home.

One such bomber is known to have been damaged by Oberfeldwebel Gerhard Reinhold, an experienced *Jagdflieger* who had come to JG 7 from II./JG 5, where he had been wounded during an operation over Paris in June 1944. Leutnant Rademacher accounted for one of the P-51 escorts near Chemnitz for his 92nd victory, but this was countered by the loss of Oberfeldwebel Heinz-Berthold Mattuschka, who fell to Mustangs over Eilenburg.

As the bombers withdrew, it was the turn of I./JG 7 to strike. Airborne from Kaltenkirchen, the *Gruppe* engaged the bombers at 1500 hrs, resulting in a claim against a B-17 for Gefreiter Heim, while Unteroffizier Harald König, formerly of JG 3, was credited with a 'probable'.

In all, JG 7 lost two pilots and two aircraft, with another two jets damaged. This was from a force of approximately 25 Me 262s on the strength of I. *Gruppe* and just under 40 aircraft from III. *Gruppe*.

On the ground, it is believed that one Me 262, piloted by Leutnant Harry Mayer, crashed in a vertical dive near Briest shortly after take-off following a technical problem. This incident perhaps highlights a reoccurring problem as reported by a representative of Messerschmitt's technical field team when he visited Brandenburg-Briest on 20 March.

Following discussions with JG 7's Technical Officer, Hauptmann Streicher, the engineer reported that pilots were struggling to master the complexities of the Me 262's controls. 'The pilots must definitely receive more training and instruction on the type' lamented the Messerschmitt man, 'especially in the cockpit of the aircraft'. And with many of the engine faults having been rectified, more aircraft were now being damaged because of undercarriage failures rather than as a result of powerplant issues. A particular problem was the weakness of the nosewheel, which was prone to collapsing.

A revealing insight into the lack of training for new Me 262 pilots was given by Leutnant Friedrich Wilhelm 'Timo' Schenk, who had been transferred to JG 7 from his post as *Staffelführer* of 2./JG 300 on 15 March;

'I had about a week to come to terms with the technology of the Me 262. Then I made three training flights in one day. As there were no two-seaters available, these were made solo, the only assistance being my radio. My fourth take off in the "thing" the next day was my first combat sortie. The conversion training of the others was at about the same pace.'

Exacerbating the training difficulties was the increasing disruption caused by Allied fighter-bombers. Such disruption forced 9. and 10./JG 7 to evacuate Oranienburg and take up residence at Parchim.

The Allied strategic air forces came again on 21 March, piling on the pressure. This time an armada of nearly 1300 heavy bombers from the Eighth Air Force targeted 12 Luftwaffe airfields across northwest Germany in an attempt to inflict damage on the jet fighter infrastructure, although 107 B-17s of the 3rd Air Division went to Plauen to bomb an armoured vehicle factory. With them came 750 P-51 escort fighters.

Simultaneously, to the south, B-24 Liberators from the Fifteenth Air Force struck at the jet airfield and facility at Neuberg.

As if this were not enough, to add to the Luftwaffe's woes, RAF Bomber Command was now operating in daylight, and it despatched 497 aircraft to bomb targets in Rheine, as well as its marshalling yards (while B-17s of the 1st Air Division struck Rheine airfield), more railways yards and a viaduct at Münster and an oil refinery in Bremen.

The *Geschwaderstab* and III./JG 7 were ordered to intercept and engage the B-17s of the 3rd Air Division at 0915 hrs over the Leipzig, Dresden and Chemnitz areas. Streaking out of misty skies northwest of Dresden in wedge formations of *Staffel* strength at 6000-7500 metres, the jets used the combined advantages of speed and surprise to evade the escort and head for the bombers, approaching from above and behind. At least six 'heavies' were claimed shot down – one each by the *Kommodore*, Major Weissenberger, and Leutnant (Fritz) Müller, Leutnant Schnörrer, Oberfähnrich Pfeiffer and Oberfeldwebel Arnold. Müller fired a short burst at one B-17 from his 30 mm cannon from a range of 300 metres, closing to 150 metres, and watched as the left wing broke away and the bomber plunged into a spin towards the earth. However, before it reached the ground the aircraft exploded.

Also flying with Weissenberger that day, and possibly for the first time operationally in an Me 262, was Major Heinrich Ehrler, who also shot down a B-17. Though Ehrler had seen service with the *Legion Condor* during the Spanish Civil War, it was with a flak unit, and his flying career commenced in 1940 when he joined 4./JG 77 in Norway.

Ehrler claimed his first victory in May of that year when he shot down a Bristol Blenheim. 4./JG 77 was designated 4./JG 5 at the beginning of February 1941, and four months later the unit commenced operations

Hauptmann Heinrich Ehrler poses for a photograph in the cockpit of his Bf 109G-2 at Petsamo, in Finland, on 27 March 1943. Subsequently promoted to major, this highly regarded 208-victory ace would eventually join the *Geschwaderstab* of JG 7 in March 1945. However, his career was dogged by past events in the Far North that troubled him, and which may, in some way, have hastened his death the following month

against the Red Air Force from bases in Norway and Finland. Ehrler's tally began to grow in early 1942, and by 22 August, when he was appointed *Staffelkapitän* of 6./JG 5, his score had climbed to 11.

In just a matter of weeks he had boosted his tally to 64 victories, and on 4 September he received the Knight's Cross. On 27 March 1943, Ehrler shot down five Russian fighters (almost certainly P-40s), and he repeated this feat on 6 June when he accounted for four Soviet Hurricanes, pushing his score to 99, with his 100th kill being claimed the following day. Six days earlier, on 1 June, he had been appointed *Kommandeur* of II./JG 5. Ehrler's trend for multiple-kills in one day was repeated on 17 March 1944 (eight) and again on 25 May (nine).

Following his 112th victory, which was achieved on 2 August 1944 (the day after he took command of *Jagdgeschwader* 5), Ehrler was awarded the Oakleaves to the Knight's Cross.

However, his spectacular career was brought sharply to an end following the events of 12 November 1944 when, in clear weather, a force of 30 Lancasters of the RAF's Nos 9 and 617 Sqns attacked the German

The Revi (Reflexvisier) 16b gunsight was a standard fitting in the cockpit of the Me 262A-1a fighter. An example is seen here in its folded-away position above and to the right of the instrument panel

The Revi (Reflexvisier) 16b gunsight raised and locked into its combat setting, looking directly through the reflector glass. The sight incorporated a sun visor, night vision filter, light bulb and dimmer switch

battleship *Tirpitz*, which was moored near Tromsö, in Norway. Ehrler's unit of Fw 190s was ordered to intercept the British bombers, but it arrived too late to prevent the *Tirpitz* from being hit by at least two 12,000-lb 'Tallboy' bombs, which caused a violent internal explosion and capsized the capital ship, killing more than half of its 1900-man crew.

Despite apparently receiving confusing radio messages as to the location of the Lancasters, Ehrler was summoned before a court-martial and held to account on the charge of being more interested in obtaining his 200th victory than guiding his fighters to their target. He was initially sentenced to death, but this was later reduced to three years' imprisonment, which, although allowing him to continue to fly, relieved him of his command. Furthermore, the award of the Swords to the Knight's Cross, for which he had been nominated, was withdrawn. In a state of some depression, he joined several of his colleagues from JG 5 in JG 7 on 27 February 1945.

Elsewhere on 21 March, a *Kette* from 9./JG 7 led by the *Staffelkapitän*, Oberleutnant Weber, made its approach towards the bombers, again from behind and slightly to the left. However, by the time Weber allowed his pilots to engage the bombers, a steady stream of return fire was already being aimed at the jets. The following moments were testimony to the lethal combination of the Me 262's firepower and speed – in more ways than one. Leutnant Ambs, flying within the *Kette*, fired a short burst at a Flying Fortress, which promptly exploded, the effect of the blast also blowing apart two other bombers in its wake. But, with no time to take evasive action, Weber few straight into the aerial inferno and perished. 'I had never seen such an explosion', Ambs recalled. 'Terrified, I pulled up and to the left'.

The second, and final, loss of the day for JG 7 came when the Me 262 of Unteroffizier Kurt Kolbe was hit by defensive fire. Two other pilots were wounded.

But the trial was not over for the Americans. Aircraft from I./JG 7 harried the bombers as they made their way home, with claims for B-17s being lodged by Leutnant Weihs and Gefreiter Heim, while Unteroffizier König accounted for a P-47 'probable'. In total, the Eighth Air Force reported seven B-17s lost following the mission, as well as nine P-51s and a P-47 from the Ninth Air Force. JG 7 listed just two Me 262s destroyed and two more damaged.

On the 22nd, 1301 bombers from the Eighth Air Force attacked military installations and airfields across northwest and central Germany, while the RAF despatched 708 sorties to bomb 'area' targets, as well as railways, fuel dumps, canals and bridges at Hildesheim, Dülmen, Dorsten, Bochholt, Bremen and Nienburg. Ominously for the Germans, from the south, the Fifteenth Air Force was becoming ever bolder, penetrating as far as the largest remaining synthetic fuel plant at Ruhland, north of Dresden, from its bases in Italy.

In an effort to repel such formidable incursions, Luftwaffe fighter controllers decided to deploy JG 7 against the Ruhland force, with III. *Gruppe* sending 27 aircraft to engage. As the jets scythed through the enemy formation at 6000 metres over the Dresden-Leipzig-Cottbus area, several bombers were hit. Victories were accredited to Leutnant Schnörrer, Oberfähnrich Pfeiffer, Oberfeldwebel Lennartz and Fähnrich Windisch. In regards to the Me 262, the last pilot recalled;

'I considered it an honour to have been selected to fly it. Comparing it to other aircraft was like comparing a Formula One racing car to a truck. Apart from the take-off and landing phases, flying the Me 262 gave me a feeling of being far superior to all others. It also gave me a feeling of safety that I had never expected, and which I had never experienced, when flying the Me 109 – an increase in the probability of survival many times over.'

Another pilot to enjoy success that day was Leutnant Viktor Petermann, who apparently was flying with JG 7 by this stage, and who held the rare and remarkable distinction of flying combat sorties with one arm.

Petermann was a true, bloodied veteran of the Eastern Front, having joined JG 52 there in June 1942. Just under a year later he had accumulated 40 victories. As an unteroffizier he flew as wingman to aces Herbert Ihlefeld and Gordon Gollob, and gained a reputation for successfully bringing his Bf 109 back to base (a distance of 100 kilometres) despite having rammed it into a Soviet I-153 biplane. Petermann also destroyed at least one enemy gunboat, and on another occasion was forced down behind Russian lines, where he evaded capture and survived exposure, dehydration and exhaustion to return to his unit.

Even more remarkable were the events of 1 October 1943 when, while returning from escorting German bombers, Petermann's Bf 109 took a direct hit from German flak in an incident of 'friendly fire'. Suffering severe wounds to his left arm and foot, and with his engine on fire, he decided to bale out of his stricken Messerschmitt. Discovering his parachute had also been damaged, Petermann belly-landed between German and Soviet lines and was rescued by Wehrmacht troops. Hospitalised for many months, the price he paid for survival was the amputation of his left arm and one of his toes.

Petermann's determination, valour and 60 aerial victories were recognised with the award of the Knight's Cross while he was still in hospital on 29 February 1944. After recovering from his wounds, he was posted to the *Reichsluftfahrtministerium*, but eventually managed to persuade those in the corridors of power to allow him to return to operational flying. Initially posted to III./JG 52, Petermann flew a Bf 109 with an artifical arm in September 1944, before joining 10./JG 52, with whom he scored another four victories in March 1945. He was subsequently posted to JG 7, although there is some debate as to the exact date he joined the *Geschwader*.

Oberfeldwebel Buchner downed a B-17 at 1300 hrs over Pretzsch on the 22nd as it made its way home, firing sustained hits into the right inboard engine and observing flames, shortly after which the bomber exploded. Oberleutnant Schall fired at a P-51 and lodged a claim for a 'probable'.

The *Geschwader Stabsschwarm*, together with 11. *Staffel*, which was airborne from Parchim, also enjoyed success north of Leipzig, with B-17s falling to the guns of Majors Weissenberger and Ehrler, Leutnant Ambs, Oberfeldwebel Arnold and Unteroffizier Köster. Leutnant Schlüter, who was one of the pilots transferred to JG 7 from *Kommando Stamp*, also downed a bomber. Finally, Leutnant Alfred Lehner, an experienced *Jagdflieger* who had joined JG 7 from II./JG 5, where he had been *Kapitän* of 3. *Staffel*, and had flown with success over Normandy, was credited with a Mustang shot down.

The tenacious Leutnant Viktor Petermann continued flying combat operations with JG 52 despite the loss of his left arm as result of severe wounds incurred over Russia. Transferring to JG 7, this indomitable Knight's Cross holder also flew the Me 262 in action, claiming at least one probable victory

Photographed from a B-17, an Me 262 sweeps past an American bomber formation. USAAF air gunners found it difficult to bring their guns to bear on such fast-moving targets

Tense groundcrew watch the activity on the airfield at Brandenburg-Briest as an armourer leans into the gun bay to work on an Me 262's four MK 108 cannon. These weapons achieved devastating results against Allied bomber formations when used to good effect by skilled pilots

With the mission over, USAAF Intelligence recorded;

'The largest jet formation, consisting of two flights of four Me 262s each, attacked the bombers north of Ruhland. The jets were flying in line abreast at 24,000 ft, and attacked from "7 o'clock high" – two bombers were reported lost to this attack. The jets were up for a second bounce, but when escort fighters turned into them, the jets split-essed to the deck. Two P-51s, returning early, were bounced by two formations of two jets each, which attacked from "12 o'clock high" and "4 o'clock level", missing the fighters and continuing on to shoot down a lone Fortress flying at 7000 ft. P-51s turned on the jets, which outdistanced them and evaded.'

The success was negated, however, by the loss of three pilots, including Feldwebel Heinz Eichner and Oberfeldwebel August Lübking, the latter another former member of JG 5 who had been credited with 35 victories. As with Joachim Weber the day before, Lübking was killed as he flew over a B-17 he had just attacked – the Flying Fortress exploded and caught Lübking in its blast. As a member of III./JG 5, Lübking had shot down an Il-2 and two Russian-flown P-40s in one mission over the Far North on 17 June 1944.

The next day, B-17s and B-24s of the Fifteenth Air Force returned to Ruhland, enduring 'moderate to intense and accurate' flak, as well as an attack by 14 Me 262s of JG 7 over Chemnitz. Major Ehrler claimed two Liberators shot down during the engagement, while Oberfeldwebel Reinhold was credited with a 'probable' over a B-17.

Further north, 117 Lancasters from RAF Bomber Command's Nos

1 and 5 Groups lost two of its number while attacking a bridge in Bremen. These were probably the victims of a group of nine Me 262s from JG 7.

The 24th was a day which dawned, according to the parlance used in a USAAF post-mission intelligence summary, with 'CAVU weather' ('Ceiling And Visibility Unlimited'). It was to be a day of maximum effort on the part of the Allied air forces in support of Operation *Varsity* – the Anglo-American airborne assault across the Rhine, which would see the largest single airborne drop in history.

The Eighth Air Force assembled a force 1714 bombers, escorted by 1300 fighters, to neutralise 18 airfields across west and northwest Germany from Vechta to Stormede and from Achmer to Ziegenhain.

While the Eighth struck the airfields, RAF Bomber Command sent a combined force of 537 Lancasters, Halifaxes and Mosquitoes to bomb marshalling yards at Sterkrade, the town of Gladbeck and benzol plants at Dortmund and Bottrop. Stretching the German defence to its limit would be a further incursion by the Fifteenth Air Force, which despatched 150 B-17s of its 5th Bomb Wing from their Italian bases to the Daimler-Benz tank engine factory in Berlin – a 2400-kilometre round trip, which was their deepest penetration raid to date.

The German piston-engined *Jagdgeschwader* were to be committed in tackling waves of fighters from the Eighth Air Force, as well as the First and Ninth Tactical Air Forces to the west, so when it became evident to their fighter controllers that the B-17s of the Fifteenth Air Force were heading north for the capital, an *Alarmstart* order was issued at 1100 hrs to 16 available jets of the *Stabsschwarm* and 11./JG 7 to intercept.

The 5th Bomb Wing had just braved a barrage of intense flak over Brux, losing four B-17s in the process, when, over Dessau, the 463rd and 483rd BGs were set upon by JG 7. The attacks were so fast that, initially, the

Oberleutnant Ernst Wörner, seen in the centre of this group holding a fir wreath following the completion of his first flight in an Me 262 in late 1944, was one of the first Luftwaffe pilots to fly the jet fighter, having transitioned from twin-engined *Zerstörer*. He was shot down and killed by P-51s while flying with 10./JG 7 on 24 March 1945. With Wörner are, to his right, the Messerschmitt test pilot, Gerd Lindner and to his left, Oberleutnant Ernst Tesch, who conducted bomb-carrying tests with the Me 262 V10 prototype

bomber gunners had no chance to range their guns as the jets flashed past them. The redoubtable Heinrich Ehrler shot down a B-17 and Oberfeldwebel Arnold claimed another, while Leutnante Rademacher and Lehner each claimed probables.

An hour later, 15 Me 262s of 9. and 10./JG 7 out of Parchim – several of them carrying R4M rockets – took on the bombers as they reached the southern outskirts of Berlin. Flying Fortresses fell to the guns of Oberleutnant Schall, Oberfeldwebel Buchner, Oberleutnant Franz Külp (a former JG 27 pilot), Leutnant Gustav Sturm (also formerly of JG 27) and Feldwebel Otto Pritzl, who had joined JG 7 from JG 3.

But once again, success came at a price. Leutnant Ambs had just attacked a B-17, and observed one wing break away from the fuselage, when his own Me 262 was hit by defensive fire. With shell splinters embedded in his face, Ambs baled out and came down in a wood near Wittenberg. Oberleutnante Franz Külp and Ernst Wörner (who was one of the original ZG 26 pilots to have converted to the Me 262) both fell victim to P-51s from either the 31st or 332nd FGs, who, together, claimed a total of eight jets shot down that day.

Also airborne with the *Gruppenstab* of I./JG 7 was Oberleutnant Walter Schuck. Along with Theo Weissenberger and Heinrich Ehrler, Schuck was one of the most successful fighter *Experten* from the Far North. He had first seen combat as a gefreiter with JG 3 in October 1940, and he eventually joined 7./JG 5 in Norway in December 1942.

Schuck did not score his first victory – a MiG 3 – until 15 May 1942, but from then on his record was meteoric. Within a year he had achieved 36 victories, but his most notable accomplishment came on 17 June 1944 when he shot down no fewer than 11 Russian aircraft in one day over Vardö and Kirkenes, in Norway – three Kittyhawks, five Il-2s, two Bostons and an Airacobra.

As an oberfeldwebel, Schuck was awarded the Knight's Cross on 8 April 1944 in recognition of his 84 victories. The Oakleaves duly followed on 30 September, by which time he had been promoted to leutnant and was in command of 7./JG 5. He was eventually transferred to JG 7 on 5 March 1945.

On 24 March, four days after his first flight in an Me 262, Schuck and his wingman engaged an F-5

Oberleutnant Walter Schuck, seen here at far left, smiles at the camera with fellow pilots of JG 5 in the Far North in June 1944. A very successful *Jagdflieger*, Schuck was awarded the Knight's Cross with Oakleaves to mark his 171st victory in September of that year. He moved to JG 7 in early March 1945 and assumed command of 3. *Staffel* at Kaltenkirchen on the 26th of that month. Schuck is seen here with three other Knight's Cross holders of JG 5, namely, from left to right, Franz Dörr, Heinrich Ehrler (later with JG 7) and 'Jockel' Norz

Lightning reconnaissance machine, escorted by two P-51s, in a draining air battle. Shortly before midday, Schuck had spotted 'three black dots' approximately 120 kilometres southwest of Berlin in the Leipzig-Dresden area. At full speed, the two Me 262s came in behind the three American aircraft and opened fire. Schuck's wingman shot down the F-5, but the Mustang pilots made every attempt to avoid their jet-powered assailants by rolling, swerving and diving. Doggedly, Schuck stayed with them and eventually chose an opportune moment to fire at each. The first P-51 blew apart in the air at 1200 hrs, while five minutes later one wing broke away from the second, which nosed over towards the earth.

Based north of Brandenburg-Briest at Parchim at this time was Leutnant Walther Hagenah of 9./JG 7. Immediately prior to joining the *Geschwader*, he had served as *Staffelkapitän* of 10.(*Sturm*)/JG 3, with whom he had shot down nine heavy bombers. Hagenah had been based at Löben, where he had been employed as an instructor for new *Sturmgruppe* pilots. Arriving at Parchim with no prior training on the Me 262, he found conditions somewhat hurried and rudimentary;

'By the time I reached JG 7, there were insufficient spare parts, insufficient engines and occasional shortages of fuel. I am sure all of these things were available somewhere, but by that stage of the war, the transport system was so chaotic that things often failed to arrive at the frontline units. We were not even allowed to look inside the cowling of the jet engines because we were told that they were secret, and we did not "need to know" what was in there!

'The danger in being sent straight to an operational unit, however, was that one could do no training if there were not enough serviceable aircraft for operations. Our "ground school" lasted for about one afternoon. We were told about the peculiarities of the jet engine, the danger of a flameout at high altitude and the poor acceleration at low altitude. Then we were told of the vital importance of handling the throttles carefully or else the engine might catch fire.

'On the day before my first flight in the Me 262, I had a brief flight in a Siebel Si 204 to practise twin-engined handling and asymmetric flying. Next morning, 25 March 1945, I made my first familiarisation flight in the rear seat of a two-seat Me 262B – precisely 17 minutes – accompanied by a weapons technician/instructor from Brandenburg-Briest. I was greatly impressed by the Me 262.

'The take-off was easy, the visibility from the cockpit was marvellous after the tail-down Bf 109 and Fw 190 and there was no torque during take-off. The only real problem I found was that when I came into land, I approached at normal speed, expecting the latter to fall away rapidly when the throttle was closed. But the Me 262 was such a clean machine. We had been warned before take-off not to throttle back to less than 6000 rpm – we were also told not to turn onto the base leg for landing at less than 300 km/h. The important thing was to make up one's mind in good time whether one was going to land or throw away that approach and try another. Because one had throttled back and the engine revolutions fell too low, they would not accelerate quickly enough if one tried to open up and go round again. Brandenburg-Briest had a concrete runway, and jets could set fire to tarmac!

'Once one began to exceed 900 km/h, the Me 262 did not "feel right" – one did not have complete control of it as it drifted from side to side, and

there was the feeling one would lose control if one took it much faster. Generally, training was unbelievably short – just an afternoon's chat and a short morning's accompanied flight, then, in the afternoon, one went solo. We had some pilots with only about 100 hours total flying time on our unit flying the Me 262. Whilst they might have been able to take-off and land the aircraft, I had the definite impression that they would have been little use in combat.'

The pilots of JG 7 were to be tested yet again the very day (25 March) that Hagenah made his maiden familiarisation flight, as 243 B-24s of the Eighth Air Force's 2nd Air Division, escorted by 223 fighters, were despatched to bomb the oil depots at Ehmen, Hitzacker and Büchen. At 0915 hrs, JG 7 was placed on readiness, and 25 minutes later 9. and 11. *Staffeln* were ordered into the air at intervals from Briest and Parchim, respectively. The first German casualty was Leutnant Günther von Rettburg, who had only recently transitioned onto jet fighters from transports. His Me 262 crashed following an engine flame-out shortly after take-off.

At 1010 hrs, the first jets made contact with the enemy over Hamburg, and the USAAF post-mission intelligence narrative recorded;

'Lead group of the Büchen force reported two passes made by four jets as the bombers uncovered for the run. Jets bored in from "6" to "7 o'clock" through the whole formation to within 100 yards or less. Lead and high squadrons of the second group were intercepted by five Me 262s between IP and the target, with attacks being made singly and in pairs from "6 o'clock" level.

'The hardest attack apparently hit the low left squadron of the group, which had become attached to a different wing on early penetration, thus resulting in the squadron being alone and six minutes late at target. Two jets attacked before the target and 15 Me 262s attacked for about ten minutes after bombing. Attacks were chiefly from "6 o'clock", mostly

Me 262A-1a 'Green 3' of the *Stab* JG 7 was probably photographed at Brandenburg-Briest. Its pilot is awaiting the signal from the groundcrewman to taxi onto the runway. This will only be given once the latter is clear of the preceding jet. Although there are similarities between this aircraft and the 'Green 3' seen in Chapter 4, either aircraft could have been a replacement for the other

level, with some high and some low. Pilots closed aggressively to within 50 yards' range – attacks were mostly singly and in pairs, although in one instance jets came in five abreast.

'The P-51s escorting this force were able to break up attacks attempted by two formations of seven jets in line astern both before and after the target, and a P-47 group supporting the same force unsuccessfully engaged six to seven Me 262s seen attacking in line abreast. However, one P-47 squadron effectively tracked one speedy jet to its Parchim base, destroying not only the chased jet but also claiming 1-0-1 on two jets which had just taken off.'

The latter may have been the Me 262s flown by Oberfähnrichs Windisch and Günther Ullrich (who had come to JG 7 from JG 27). Both pilots had just downed a bomber when they were attacked by the fighter escorts. Using their superior speed, the German pilots attempted to escape back to Parchim. Windisch made it, but Ullrich was caught by the American fighters, possibly from the 56th FG, which had pursued the jets all the way home. Strafed as he made his landing approach, Ullrich endeavoured to jump from his burning aircraft at a height of just 250 metres, but he was too low for his parachute to deploy and he fell to his death.

A similar fate befell Oberleutnant Schätzle, the former bomber pilot being attacked by fighters as he attempted to land at Rechlin-Lärz. Like Ullrich, he jumped out of his burning machine, but he was dead by the time he hit the ground.

US Intelligence noted poignantly;

Oberleutnant Schätzle joined JG 7 from the Luftwaffe bomber force. He is seen here sitting in the cockpit of Me 262A-1a Wk-Nr. 110997. On 24 March 1945, he was killed as he landed his jet at Rechlin-Lärz when he came under attack by American fighters

'One jet was chased to Rechlin and destroyed. This day's operations focus attention on the importance of hitting enemy jets when they are low – landing or taking off – preferably on take-off. Once jets are at operational height, opportunities for our fighters are greatly decreased, and the task of close escort made increasingly difficult.'

At least four German pilots did manage to get through to the bombers to execute successful attacks or claim enemy fighters shot down. Oberleutnant Schall and Leutnant Schnörrer each shot down a P-51, while Leutnant Rademacher claimed a *Herrausschüss* over a B-24 and Leutnant Fritz Müller and Oberfeldwebel Buchner shot down a Liberator apiece near Lüneburg and Hamburg, respectively. Müller's victory was gained at a price though, for he was hit by return fire in his port engine, forcing him to land at Stendal, where he crashed into a Ju 88 parked in a hangar.

Former *Transportflieger* Feldwebel Fritz Taube found himself alone shortly after take-off, having lost contact with the rest of his comrades from 10./JG 7. Nevertheless, he managed to bring down a Liberator at 1030 hrs, shooting off its port-side wing. Minutes later, however, Taube was set upon by Mustangs from above. His jet took hits to the fuel tank and exploded in mid-air.

1. *Jagddivision* later reported having deployed some 25 Me 262s of JG 7 against the bombers, with the *Geschwader* claiming seven aircraft destroyed and two probables. In return, four pilots were lost and a further five posted missing.

The grim bloodletting continued during the final days of the month, despite generally inclement weather conditions. On the 27th, Major

A maintenance NCO of JG 7 glances down at the camera from the port wing of Me 262A-1a Wk-Nr. 110997 at Brandenburg-Briest in February 1945. This Leipheim-built jet was delivered to JG 7 on 16 January 1945, but it was soon found to be suffering from technical problems. The fighter was damaged while serving with I. *Gruppe* on 15 February, having suffered yet another technical failure

Rudorffer led a formation of jets from I./JG 7 against a raid by 115 Lancasters of the RAF's No 5 Group that had been sent to bomb oil storage tanks at Farge, near Bremen. Although Leutnant Günther Heckmann of 1. *Staffel* duly claimed a Lancaster shot down, Bomber Command recorded no losses.

The next day, the targets for the Americans were Berlin, Stendal and Hannover. I./JG 7, led by Oberleutnant Grünberg, was again in the fray, engaging re-routed Flying Fortresses near Stendal. Oberleutnant Stehle, *Staffelkapitän* of 2./JG 7, claimed a B-17 and a P-51, while Oberleutnant Schuck shot down a P-51 for his 201st victory. Damage was inflicted on Fähnrich-Feldwebel Heinrich Janssen's Me 262 of 3./JG 7, which received a number of severe hits in its left engine, forcing the pilot to disengage.

On 30 March it was the turn of the north German ports to be targeted, with U-boat yards and oil storage tanks at Hamburg, Bremen, Wilhelmshaven and Farge all being bombed. This time the USAAF sent a colossal armada of 1320 bombers to do the work, protected by no fewer than 852 fighters.

To meet the enemy, I. and III./JG 7 could call on just under 40 serviceable Me 262s, but when they were given the *Alarmstart* order,

A maintenance NCO clambers down from the wing of I./JG 7's Me 262A-1a Wk-Nr. 110997 at Brandenburg-Briest in February 1945. This unlucky aircraft was eventually struck off JG 7's inventory on the 16th of that month due to its history of unacceptable performance, the jet duly being stripped down for parts

three aircraft failed on take-off and another three had to return to base shortly after due to engine or undercarriage failure. Twelve Me 262s of I./JG 7 searched in vain for the enemy formation, having been given incorrect directions by ground control, leaving just 19 machines to engage the massive USAAF formation – results are not known. Refuelled, the jets made a second attempt to attack the bombers in the early afternoon.

Contact was made north of Lüneburg, and despite a hail of defensive fire, Leutnant Petermann claimed a probable, while Leutnant Schnörrer scored two victories over B-17s at 1330 hrs –

On 30 March 1945, Leutnant Karl Schnörrer, commander of 11./JG 7 and former wingman to Walter Nowotny, downed two B-17s over northwest Germany. His fighter was hit by the defensive fire from a third bomber, and as he broke away from the formation, he was chased down by P-51s. Forced to bale out, Schnörrer struck the tail unit of his stricken fighter and badly injured his legs for the second time. He did not fly again during the war

his last of the war. However, as he pulled away from the scene of combat, his jet was hit by machine gun fire from the bomber formation. Turning for home, Schnörrer was chased by P-51s, and he decided that the best course of action would be to bale out of his damaged fighter. In doing so, he struck the tail unit and – once again – badly injured his legs. Despite this, Schnörrer managed to land by parachute.

Major Rudorffer led a small group of Me 262s of I./JG 7 up from Kaltenkirchen, intercepting more bombers over Hamburg. Rudorffer claimed two of the escort fighters, while Gefreiter Heim accounted for another and Flieger Reiher destroyed a B-17.

In a separate incident, Unteroffizier Heiner Geisthövel attempted to shoot down one of several Mosquitoes conducting a radio counter-measures flight. Although he was able to fire a good burst at the Mosquito, no such aircraft was listed as lost by the RAF. The unfortunate Geisthövel was literally chased to the ground on his way home, being strafed by three P-51s as he came in to land at Kaltenkirchen. Although he survived the attack, Leutnant Erich Schulte, who scrambled with another pilot in an effort to fend off the Mustangs, perished when his fighter was shot down not far from the airfield. Two members of the groundcrew were also killed as Geisthövel came in.

Yet it was not just the airfields that were exposed. At 1035 hrs, USAAF fighters carried out a low-level attack against three lorries belonging to JG 7 on a secton of *Autobahn* near Wunstorf. One vehicle was destroyed, but there were no casualties.

That day, in a reflection of the prevailing conditions, *Luftflotte Reich* issued orders to the effect that to maintain operational serviceability of jet-propelled units, 'no alterations in personnel to be made. No training for ground fighting or other duties to be carried out. No women to be employed'.

The last day of March 1945 would see another major effort in the relentless Allied strategic bombing offensive. While the Eighth Air

Force struck at oil refineries at Zeitz and Bad Berka, as well as other targets in Brandenburg, Gotha, Stendal, Salzwedel, Braunschweig and Halle, RAF Bomber Command focused on the Blohm und Voss shipyards in Hamburg. A force of 469 Lancasters, Halifaxes and Mosquitoes arrived over a cloud-covered target area, but still bombed, inflicting considerable damage to the southern districts of the port city.

Against this raid, 2. *Jagddivision* deployed some 20 jets from I. and III./JG 7, with Oberleutnant Stehle (on the first of two sorties he would fly this day) leading the first wave of 12 aircraft against Lancasters as they came in over Bremen. Stehle was followed by another wave led by Oberleutnant Grünberg that was sent to engage more bombers already in the Hamburg area, while Me 262s from 9. and 10./JG 7 followed.

On this occasion, fortune was to favour the defenders as, in addition to 30 mm cannon shells, repeated salvos of R4M missiles streaked into the British formation. For the crews of the Lancasters, the German skies became a scene of smoke-blackened carnage as bombers exploded and shattered wings and engines spun away from fuselages. Hermann Buchner recalled what happened after the rockets had been fired;

'I made a right turn and lined up for another attack. This was made using the nose cannon. My Lancaster lay directly in my sights and I only had to get a bit closer. Now, I opened fire, the hits were good, but the pilot of the Lancaster must have been an old hand. He turned his Lancaster steeply over on its right wing, making a tight turn around the main axis. With my speed, I was unable to see if my shots had had any effect, or to see how he flew on. I had to think about returning home. The other pilots were also having the same problem. We had a shortage of fuel.'

This first attack resulted in 13 bombers being shot down, with double scores lodged by Oberleutnante Stehle, Grünberg and Schall, Leutnante Hans Todt (who had joined JG 7 earlier in the month from 8./JG 301, where he had accumulated ten victories) and Schenk and Fähnrich Friedrich Ehrig, while Flieger Reiher and Leutnant Weihs also made claims – but the day was not over.

Later that afternoon, Stehle led a second attack by 2./JG 7 against Lancasters over Osnabrück, shooting one down to add to his two earlier victories, while aircraft from the *Stabsschwarm* and 11. *Staffel* engaged B-17s and B-24s over the American targets. Five *Viermots* and two escort fighters were claimed, accredited to Majors Weissenberger and Ehrler (a P-51 probable for his 206th victory), Leutnant Rademacher (a P-51 for his 95th victory), Oberfähnrich Windisch and Oberfeldwebel Pritzl, while 2. *Jagddivision* reported one jet lost.

The achievement of 31 March may have offered a welcome boost to the outnumbered jet pilots, but the great superiority of the Allied air forces was undeniable. The question, however, was just how long the battle could be maintained flying an aircraft that was difficult to master, challenging to maintain and crewed by weary and mostly under-trained pilots who suffered from shortages of fuel and parts that depended on a badly disrupted transport system to reach them. The following weeks would require every measure of resolve the handful of more experienced jet pilots possessed.

DESTRUCTION

On 1 April 1945, Adolf Hitler relocated his headquarters from the Chancellery building in Berlin to a deep bunker complex just behind it. It was a move redolent of defeat. In Moscow that same day, Josef Stalin airily enquired of his commanders, 'Well now. Who is going to take Berlin, we or the Allies?'

In a touch of irony, in Hamburg, the *Reichsführer*-SS, Heinrich Himmler, told local officials that it would be the disagreements between the Allied powers, as well as the imminent appearance of new jet aircraft in large numbers, that would save Germany. Yet for the men of JG 7, this would have sounded like a hollow prediction. The *Geschwader* had taken delivery of 89 new Me 262s during March – by far the greatest share of the 120 machines delivered to the various jet units. However, it was a paltry amount compared to Allied resources. Nevertheless, the demands placed on JG 7 were about to become greater than ever.

Furthermore, the first seeds of decay in any form of coherent fighter defence leadership were being sown. Command was already fragmented and competitive. In one quarter, from the headquarters of the IX.(J) *Fliegerkorps* at Treuenbrietzen, the former bomber commander

By the spring of 1945, a considerable quantity of Me 262s was being produced by so-called 'Waldwerk' forest factories. These were assembly facilities deliberately dispersed to secret, often rural and isolated, locations in an attempt to foil the effectiveness of Allied bombing. Although relatively primitive, and often manned by slave labour, they nevertheless made a significant contribution to total Me 262 production. Here, two virtually completed jets have been abandoned beneath camouflage drapes at one such facility deep in a pine forest somewhere in Germany

Generalmajor Dietrich Peltz was consolidating his position as commander of all of the bomber units now struggling to familiarise themselves with the Me 262 fighter, directing these units in the aerial defence of parts of Holland and Denmark, as well as Austria and Bohemia-Moravia. Peltz's sentiments at this time are made clear from an intercepted radio message dated 3 April;

'Peltz reports work on many airfields not being carried out with necessary energy. Half of the working day of 12 hours is wasted as a result of Allied air raids. Work is to be started before first light, any rest to be taken during main raid period and work resumed at night. Divisional commanders to report if this arrangement not practical or if repair of runways and tracks takes too long. Unit commanders to report to the Division or to Peltz personally if work is not carried out by the station commander in the spirit of this order.'

A further indication of Peltz's growing influence in fighter operations can be seen from the fact that the two fighter divisions subordinate to *Luftflotte* 4 and *Luftwaffenkommando West* were now ordered to 'maintain close contact' with IX.(J) *Fliegerkorps*.

At this point, the SS began to 'move in'. In southern Germany, Luftwaffe motor transport was being put at the disposal of Hitler's personal Plenipotentiary for Jet Aircraft Production and Operational Deployment, SS-*Obergruppenführer und General der Waffen*-SS Dr.Ing. Hans Kammler.

Curious American soldiers examine the intricacies of a Jumo 004 turbojet in the final assembly area of a 'Waldwerk' somewhere in southern Germany. Although the building appears quite primitive in its construction, inside, mass production techniques – such as rail-mounted trolleys – ensured that the plant performed efficiently. Many aircraft delivered to JG 7 would have come from such facilities

An Me 262A-1a Wk-Nr. 111918 of the *Gruppenstab* I./JG 7, as found abandoned by American troops in western Germany

Towards the end of March, Hitler had ordered that Kammler was to command all necessary development, testing and production of jet aircraft, and to coordinate all neccesary logistic operations previously handled by the Minister for Armaments and War Production. He was also to assume command of jet production through to operational deployment. According to Hitler's decree. 'Kammler is placed under my personal command and has my fullest authority. All Commands of the Wehrmacht, Party and Reich organisations are to assist him in the execution of his duties and are to carry out his orders'.

On 3 April, Dr Goebbels wrote in his dairy;

'The *Führer* has had very prolonged discussions with *Obergruppenführer* Kammler, who now carries responsibility for the reform of the Luftwaffe. Kammler is doing excellently, and great hopes are placed on him. At the daily briefing conferences, the Luftwaffe comes in for the sharpest criticism from the *Führer*. Day after day, Göring has to listen without being in a position to demur at all.'

It was against such a backdrop that JG 7 now fought its war. On the 1st, as the *Führer* had moved into his bunker, I./JG 7 left its base at Kaltenkirchen for airfields that were deemed safer. 1. *Staffel* flew to Brandenburg-Briest, which had been vacated by Generalleutnant Galland's JV 44 (the latter had moved south to Munich-Riem), while 2. *Staffel* went to Burg and 3. *Staffel* to Oranienburg.

The next day, bad weather conditions kept the Eighth Air Force from its airfield targets in occupied Denmark, and the raid was aborted at the Danish coast. Despite this, Oberfeldwebel Buchner of 10./JG 7 brushed with a lone Spitfire over Hamburg and almost collided with it. He had approached the British aircraft at too high a speed, veered away too sharply and momentarily lost control of his fighter. The Spitfire disappeared.

On the 3rd, 719 B-17s and B-24s bombed the U-boat yards at Kiel, as well as Flensburg airfield. The Luftwaffe mounted no significant defence, but the Americans did report observing small numbers of jets in the target area – whether these were from JG 7 is not known. That evening, I./JG 7 is recorded as having 33 Me 262s, while III. *Gruppe* reported 27 (just under two thirds of its 'on paper' strength).

The events of 4 April were very different. While RAF Bomber Command sent 243 Lancasters to attack the town of Nordhausen, 950 Flying Fortresses and Liberators drawn from all but one of the Eighth Air Force's bomber groups set out to target the vacated field at Kaltenkirchen and 11./JG 7's base at Parchim, as well as the airfields at Perleberg, Wesendorf, Fassberg, Hoya, Dedelsdorf and Eggebeck. U-boat yards at Finkenwarder and shipyards at Kiel were also targeted. The bombers were protected by a force of some 800 escort fighters.

The B-24s of the 2nd Air Division led the formation, crossing the German coast west of Heide at 0900 hrs. However, Kaltenkirchen was found to be covered in cloud, so mid-way between Hamburg and Lübeck, the formation split, with the lead combat wing making for Parchim while elements of the rest of the formation either turned for home or made course for Perleberg.

Some 15-20 jets of III./JG 7, led by Major Rudolf Sinner, took off at 0915 hrs. As they did so, the P-51s of the 339th FG, which were conducting a sweep ahead of the B-24s, appeared over Parchim. It was a very unfortunate scenario for the Me 262s, as they had been caught at their most vulnerable moment.

Major Rudolf Sinner, erstwhile *Kommandeur* of III./JG 7, walks away from hospital with his head bandaged to protect the injuries he suffered following his bale-out on 4 April 1945. In the Me 262, Sinner had been 'pleased and proud to be made responsible for the testing and operation in combat of a new, greatly promising and interesting weapon'

As Sinner climbed through the cloud in his rocket-laden jet, he spotted Mustangs diving towards him, but found it impossible to adopt an evasive manouevre due to his proximity to the ground. He attempted to fire off his R4Ms to lose weight, but the firing mechanism had failed, and seconds later his jet was shot up by the eight P-51s now pursuing him. With flames licking into his cockpit, Sinner managed a slight turn and baled out. Although he avoided contact with the tail surfaces, his right leg had become entangled in his parachute harness and lines. Spinning through the air, he landed in a field, but remained connected to his parachute, which dragged him along for several metres into a barbed wire fence. According to Sinner, the American fighters strafed him while he was on the ground, but eventually he was able to run for the cover of a ploughed furrow.

Suffering from severe burns to the head and hands, Sinner was taken to hospital. 4 April was to be his 305th, and last, combat mission. A new *Kommandeur* would have to be found for III./JG 7.

Meanwhile, the other Me 262s of III. *Gruppe* struggled to avoid the Mustangs, with five jets being shot down in the space of minutes, resulting in the loss of the JG 5 veterans Leutnant Lehner and Oberfeldwebel Reinhold, as well as Unteroffizier Otto Heckmann. Two other pilots were lost, but their identities remain unknown. Six Me 262s attracted damage, but they lost the P-51s in the cloud and landed at other airfields. The USAAF recorded that despite the attack by the escort,

A scene of carnage in the skies over Hamburg as a B-24 Liberator of the 448th BG breaks up in mid-air following an attack by Me 262s of JG 7 on 4 April 1945

scattered attacks did continue against the bombers until the target was reached at 0937 hrs. By the time the B-24s had left Parchim, however, the airfield installations had been badly damaged, including a vital spare parts storage facility.

Meanwhile, 25 Me 262s of 9. and 10./JG 7, some armed with R4Ms, took off in elements of four between 0915-0920 hrs from Brandenburg-Briest, Burg and Lärz and made contact with the incoming bombers heading for Perleberg, south of Bremen. The jets managed to drive their way through the P-47 escort and hack down several *Viermots* using cannon and rockets, opening fire with their R4Ms from 600 metres. Immediately, several Liberators took hits, with debris flying through the air as they veered away from their formation. The USAAF noted that;

'Some 25-30 jets in three waves were sighted heading west by fighters escorting the Perleberg force immediately after the turn onto the bomb run. Escorts prevented all but the first wave of eight from hitting the bombers in formation. After the first coordinated attack, Me 262s darted through the formation in individual passes, and at the target some ten jets closed in from all directions. A running engagement ensued from 0940 to 0955 hrs and two B-24s were shot down for claims of 2-0-13 against the jets.'

In fact, six Liberators did not return from this mission, with claims being made by Major Weissenberger, Oberleutnant Stehle, Leutnante Fritz Müller, Rademacher and Schenk, Feldwebel Pritzl and Fähnrich Pfeiffer, while Gefreiter Heim claimed a probable. Oberleutnant Schall and Leutnant Weihs shot down a P-51 and a P-47, respectively, but Schall was forced to bale out near Parchim shortly afterwards.

As the B-24s unloaded their bombs over Perleberg, one Me 262 was apparently shot down by 1Lt Michael J Kennedy of the 4th FG, who was flying his P-51D *Lil Aggie*. He reported;

'We were escorting a box of B-24s when all of a sudden eight Me 262s attacked our bombers. Two of the jets pulled up after making their pass, two others pulled the old '109 tactic of doing a split-S after their pass and the other four used little or no evasive action. I was at 18,000 ft at the time, and picked out one that started a gradual descent in a gentle starboard turn. Having run into '262s before, I started down after him, leading the German pilot quite a bit.

'For what seemed a very long time I pointed my aircraft at a non-existent point hoping that I had planned correctly. Then, all of a sudden, it happened. I had increased my air speed, gained on him and I was on his tail at extreme K-14 gunsight range. I opened fire and immediately observed strikes in the wing and the right engine nacelle. The right jet disintegrated and I flew through some of the bits and pieces and began to overrun the aeroplane. I pulled off power, dumped combat flaps and went right on by him. I pulled into a tight port orbit, and just as I started to pull around, my wingman informed me that the Me 262 had exploded. I'd fired 607 rounds of Armour-Piercing Incendiary ammunition.'

Despite having downed eight USAAF aircraft, at the end of the day, Major Weissenberger was forced to report that five of his pilots had been killed or were missing, three were wounded and 23 jets had suffered battle damage or were in need of repair. The *Geschwader* was now finding it difficult to cope.

Me 262s of 11./JG 7 undergo maintenance between missions at Brandenburg-Briest in early April 1945. Such a scene was a priority target for free-ranging USAAF fighter pilots

Badly battered, JG 7 was able to mount only a limited response to the USAAF raids of 5 and 6 April. On the latter date, 646 B-17s and B-24s set out to bomb railway targets at Halle, Eisleben, Leipzig and Gera, escorted by almost the same number of fighters. According to the USAAF, its bomber crews sighted just two Me 262s near Halle, and they did not engage, while its fighter pilots also saw two – one at Halle and one near Leipzig. Nevertheless, the Eighth Air Force lost four B-17s that day, and Major Heinrich Ehrler is known to have shot down (or at least damaged) two bombers, taking his final tally to 208 victories, prior to being killed.

There is some conjecture as to the facts surrounding Ehrler's death, including the theory that, in some way, he felt obligated to redeem himself for events discussed in the previous chapter. Whatever the case, it is known that following his encounter with the B-17s, Ehrler was reported shot down by a P-51 northeast of Schaarlippe. The official loss document, signed by Weissenberger, gives the date as 6 April 1945, but no combat with Me 262s was reported by the Americans on that date. For this reason, it is possible that, in fact, the combat took place two days earlier.

One German report on the action stated that just before he died, Ehrler radioed to Weissenberger, 'Theo, I've just used all my ammunition. I'm going to ram! See you in Valhalla!' However, Ehrler's death certificate, signed by both Weissenberger and Schuck, stated simply that he failed to return from a mission, and that his body had been located near Stendal.

Meanwhile, the war against the bombers was about to reach desperate new heights. Following a request from Göring in early March 1945 for volunteers to take part in a radical operation 'from which there is little possibility of returning', a small group of pilots arrived in great secrecy at

91

The fact that it was forbidden for any Luftwaffe personnel to photograph or film Me 262s makes these atmospheric and covert film stills (seen on pages 91-93) even more remarkable. Here, an Me 262A-1a of 11./JG 7 is filmed parked off the runway at Brandenburg-Briest on 7 April 1945

Stendal on the 24th to begin training as part of the so-called *Schulungslehrgang 'Elbe'*, known also as *Sonderkommando 'Elbe'*. This was the brainchild of ever-inventive Oberst Hajo Herrmann, bomber ace and founder of the relatively successful *Wilde Sau* nightfighter units in 1943.

Herrmann's plan was to assemble a group of pilots who would be prepared to fly their fighters in a massed attack against a large Allied bomber formation using conventional armament, but also with the intent of ramming enemy *Viermots* to bring them down. The chances of survival would be slim, but Herrmann was encouraged by the initial call for volunteers.

Purportedly, he soon had 2000 names, and agreement from Göring that 1500 fighters – mainly Bf 109G/Ks – would be made available for the operation, which was to be codenamed *Wehrwolf*. There is no record of any of JG 7's pilots volunteering for this mission – and in the event that they had, it seems unlikely that the Luftwaffe would have allowed any of its valuable jet-trained pilots to participate.

The operation was finally launched on 7 April against an Eighth Air Force formation of 1261 bombers attacking jet airfields and marshalling yards in northern and central Germany. As Herrmann's force commenced their attack, a total of 59 Me 262s – 44 from III./JG 7 and 15 from I./KG(J) 54 – clashed with the American fighter escort in an attempt to draw them away from the bombers. Sadly for the young volunteers, the jet force was too small to prevent the destruction of 59 of its fighters by the American escort, with a further 40 being claimed by the bomber gunners between the Dummer and Steinhuder Lakes.

Two bombers were, however, claimed by pilots from III./JG 7, who broke through the fighter escort in their R4M-armed Me 262s – a B-17

over Parchim by Oberfeldwebel Göbel and a B-24 near Bremen by Unteroffizier Schöppler. Oberfeldwebel Buchner fired all his rockets but found that the defensive fire was so intense that he was unable to observe whether he had hit his target or not.

Buchner and his fellow pilots were unable to return to Parchim, so they were ordered to Wismar instead, but when they reached that airfield they discovered it was already under attack by Thunderbolts. Low on fuel, they were forced to land and quickly abandon their jet fighters on the grass, exposed, as the P-47s strafed some nearby Ju 52/3ms. The jets survived only because the drifting smoke from the burning transports obscured them from the piston-engined predators.

Later, two P-51s were claimed by Oberfähnrich Neumann and Fähnrich Pfeiffer from the same unit, while Oberleutnant Schuck, by now serving as *Staffelkapitän* of 3./JG 7 at Oranienburg, shot down a P-51 in the early afternoon near Wittenberge. The Eighth Air Force returned to England with 17 of its bombers lost and a further 188 badly damaged.

Oberfeldwebel Buchner was in the air again the next day at 1100 hrs with at least one *Schwarm* from 10./JG 7 when 1103 bombers struck at airfield and transport targets in central and southern Germany. The formation of jets swept through the fighter escort to attack B-17s over Bremen – probably those of the 1st Air Division heading for Stendal and Halberstadt. The pilots of 10. *Staffel* observed hits and also saw the telltale signs of black smoke, but were unable to linger around the formation due to the reacting escort. Oberleutnant Stehle is believed to have led more Me 262s of I./JG 7 against other USAAF bombers, but precisely where and with what result is not clear. A P-38 and a pair of P-51s were also claimed by Leutnant Weihs and Unteroffizier Geisthövel, respectively.

The hazy figure of a member of the groundcrew uses his boot to apply pressure to the nosewheel of an Me 262 of 11./JG 7 at Brandenburg-Briest again on 7 April 1945. By this stage of the war it was a considerable risk for the pilots and groundcrews of the Luftwaffe's jet fighter units to perform such basic maintenance in the open, such was the threat from prowling Allied fighters

93

Having transitioned to the Me 262 from a ground-attack unit, Oberfeldwebel Hermann Buchner proved himself a potent jet fighter pilot by scoring several victories in the aircraft while with JG 7. Buchner was awarded the Knight's Cross in July 1944 for 46 aerial victories – an extraordinary score for a *Schlact* pilot

On the 9th the RAF came, sending 57 Lancasters from No 5 Group to bomb oil storage and U-boat pens in Hamburg, with some aircraft carrying devastating 'Grand Slam' and 'Tallboy' bombs. A force of 29 Me 262s from JG 7 engaged the bombers, flying through heavy defensive fire, to lodge claims for four Lancasters, although only two are listed by the RAF as having been lost. Those pilots claiming were Oberleutnant Schall, Gefreiter Paul Müller, Leutnant Rudolf Zingler and Unteroffizier Günther Engler, while Leutnant Fritz Müller accounted for a P-47.

That day, *Luftflotte Reich* reported *Stab*/JG 7 at Brandenburg-Briest as having five Me 262s on strength, with four serviceable. I./JG 7 at Brandenburg, Burg and Oranienburg, under the acting command of Oberleutnant Fritz Stehle, had 41 aircraft, of which 26 were serviceable. Finally, III./JG 7 at Parchim, Oranienburg, Lärz and Brandenburg, led by the recently appointed Knight's Cross holder and replacement for Rudolf Sinner, Major Wolfgang Späte, had a total of 30 jets, of which 23 were serviceable.

Until March 1945, Späte had commanded JG 400 – the only unit to fly the volatile Me 163 rocket-powered interceptor on an operational basis in defence of German oil refineries. However, lacking the specialised rocket fuel needed for their engines, suitably trained pilots and transport, JG 400 had been wound down, with the *Geschwaderstab* being dissolved, I./JG 400 disbanded and its personnel sent to the infantry and the remaining *Staffeln* scattered across Germany.

Späte, one of Germany's best known pre-war glider pilots, a holder of the Oakleaves to the Knight's Cross and with more than 90 victories to his name (gained mainly in Russia, where he had flown with JG 54), temporarily found himself redundant. As he later recalled;

'Gollob, as successor to Galland, telephoned me and asked how I wished to be employed from then on. When I explained that I wished to defend my Fatherland by flying the Me 262, he said "Okay – JG 7 or JV 44?" I decided to go to JG 7. I chose the latter because I knew the unit had sufficient aircraft, enough fuel and the *Geschwaderkommodore*,

Although of hazy quality, this photograph offers a rare view of Me 262s of 11./JG 7 taxiing at Brandenburg-Briest in early April 1945. The very different styles of colour finish are evident

Theo Weissenberger, was a friend of mine from the time when we both participated as glider pilots in soaring competitions on the Wasserkuppe long before the war. It was also widely known that JG 7 had achieved considerable successes. I thought it would offer me the best opportunity to engage myself in the final defence of our country.'

The following day, 10 April, would see a dramatic escalation in the 'jet war' in terms of deployment and commitment on behalf of JG 7's pilots. No fewer than 1232 B-17s and B-24s of the Eighth Air Force were active directly over the *Geschwader's* zone of operations, bringing nearly 900 fighters with them. It was as if the Allied planners were deliberately provoking the jets to come up and fight against such overwhelming odds.

The targets were airfields, transport hubs and a military infrastructure centre at Oranienburg, Rechlin, Neuruppin, Stendal, Brandenburg-Briest, Zerbst, Burg, Parchim and Wittenberge. The respective *Staffeln* of JG 7 had been placed at readinesss during the morning, and the German raid reporting system began plotting the incursion after midday.

However, the first damage to JG 7 was not sustained in the air, but on the ground at Burg, where at least three of the *Geschwader's* Me 262s were destroyed in the bombing. The raid was to prove catastrophic for the German units based there, with hangars and workshops either being destroyed or badly damaged, and at least 200 bombs fell on the runways and taxi-tracks. Many aircraft were also destroyed, including a number of Bf 109/Ju 88 *'Mistel'* combinations needed for operations on the Oder Front. The scale of damage is illustrated by the fact that the relatively rare *'Mistel'* were also within the total of 29 aircraft destroyed and 45 damaged at Rechlin, while another five such combinations were wrecked at Oranienburg.

Just after 1400 hrs, as the Americans pulled away from Burg, Me 262s of 9. and 10./JG 7 took off from Parchim once more in less that perfect weather conditions, with pouring rain and visibility down to 2000

metres. As the cloud hung at 150-200 metres, the take-off was staggered to avoid accidents and collisions. But even amidst such conditions, the American fighters were ever-present, hounding the jets as they attempted to lift off the ground. P-51s swooped down on the Me 262s flown by Fähnrich Windisch and Unteroffizier Louis-Peter Vigg, raking them with machine gun fire. Both pilots were rescued from the smouldering wreckage of their fighters.

Half-an-hour later, the bombs from the B-24s of the 2nd Air Division fell on Parchim, narrowly missing the airfield itself to fall on open ground, although some buildings and personnel were killed in the attack.

Shortly after the Parchim force had taken off, a further 30 Me 262s were scrambled out of Oranienburg, Rechlin-Lärz and Brandenburg-Briest. This force was directed to take on the bombers of the 1st Air Division that the German fighter controllers thought – wrongly – were heading for Berlin. Among an element of pilots from 9. *Staffel* was Walther Hagenah, who recalled;

Assigned to the *Geschwaderstab* of JG 7, this Me 262A-1a was filmed taxiing past at Brandenburg-Briest on 7 April 1945. Note the very unusual 'tortoise shell' camouflage scheme and the tactical number '2' just visible below the running fox emblem of JG 7 painted in its customary position on the nose of the aircraft, just forward of the cockpit

This Me 262 has the tactical number 'Green 2' and chevron and bar fuselage markings of the *Geschwader* Operations Officer of JG 7, although it is possible that it may even have been another machine assigned to the *Kommodore*, Major Weissenberger, at Brandenburg-Briest in April 1945

Leutnant Walther Hagenah had served as *Staffelkapitän* of 10.(*Sturm*)/JG 3 and then on the *Stab* of that *Gruppe*, before joining 9./JG 7. He was 'greatly impressed' by the Me 262

'The *Gruppe* had just moved from Parchim to Lärz, and although we had a full establishment of 30 aircraft, only about half of them were serviceable. Enemy bombers had been observed moving in to attack Berlin, and my unit was one of those ordered to engage them. But during start-up, my right engine refused to light and I had to stay behind. It took the technicians about 15 minutes to get the engine running and then, with another Me 262 flown by a young feldwebel, I took off late to engage the bombers.

'We received no instructions from the ground when airborne – our task was merely to "engage bombers over Berlin". Once above cloud at about 5000 metres, I could see the bomber formation clearly at about 6000 metres. I was flying at about 550 km/h in a slight climb after them. Everything seemed to be going fine. In 3-4 minutes we would be with the bombers. Then, as an experienced fighter pilot, I had the old "tingling at the back of the neck" feeling that perhaps enemy fighters were about.

'I had a good look around, and in front and above I saw six Mustangs passing above me from almost head-on. At first I thought they had not seen me, and so I continued on. But, just to be on the safe side, I glanced back once more – and it was a good thing for me that I did, because at that moment I saw the Mustangs diving down and curving round on to the pair of us. With the speed of their dive, and the speed we had lost because of our climb, they stood a good chance of catching us. Then they opened fire and tracer began to flash disconcertingly close to our aircraft.

'I opened my throttle fully and put my nose down a little to increase my own speed, and resolved to outrun the enemy fighters. I did not attempt to throw off their aim – I knew the moment I turned my speed would fall, and then they would have me. I told the feldwebel on my left to keep going, but obviously he became scared because I noticed him weaving from side to side, then he turned away to the left.

'It was just what the Mustang pilots wanted, and in no time they had broken off from me and were on to him. His aircraft received several hits and I saw it go down and crash – my companion was unable to bale out. I kept an eye on the enemy fighters at 4000 metres and watched them reform and turn round to fly westwards for home.

'Feeling vengeful, I decided to have a go at them. I rapidly closed in on them from behind, but at a range of about 500 metres the Mustang leader started rocking his wings and I knew I had been seen. If I continued I knew that the enemy fighters would probably split up into two and curve round from either side onto my tail, so I resolved to strike first. I loosed off all 24 of the R4M rockets under my wings straight at the enemy fighters and I was very lucky – I hit two of them and they went down out of control. This time I had plenty of speed, and had little trouble in avoiding the fire from their companions.

'But I had no time for self-congratulation, because my own fuel was beginning to run short and I had to get down as soon as I could. I picked up a beacon on my receiver and found that it was the airfield at Köthen. I called up the airfield on the radio and I said I wanted to land there, but they called back and warned me to be careful as there were *'Indiana'* (enemy fighters) over the field.

'When I arrived, I saw that there were enemy fighters about trying to strafe the field, but the light flak defences were giving them a hard time

and I managed to slip in unnoticed. Suddenly, however, it seems I *was* noticed, because almost as one, the Mustangs packed up and went home – perhaps they thought my own and other jet fighters had come to tackle them. Certainly they did not know I was short of fuel. I made a tight, curving approach and hurled the Messerschmitt onto the runway, breathing a sigh of relief at having got down safely. But then the Mustangs must have realised what was going on and in a trice they were back over the airfield, and it was my turn to have a rough time. Fortunately for me, the flak defences were still on their toes, and I was not hit.'

The rest of the German force hit the B-17s of the 1st Air Division as it reached its actual targets of Oranienburg and Rechlin. From the American perspective, it was more of the same;

'The lead and second groups were first hit by a total of about 12 Me 262s, which attacked singly and in pairs, pressing their attacks closely, and in some cases flying right through the formation. Enemy aircraft were very aggressive and daring, attacking from the tail, level and above, closing to within very short distances. From these attacks the 1st Air Division lost five B-17s to enemy aircraft and claimed 7-1-8 Me 262s. Fighter escort was reported to have done an excellent job of breaking up any formations before they could get through to the bombers.'

Despite the escort screen, Oberleutnant Walter Schuck, leading seven Me 262s of 3./JG 7 in his 'Yellow 1', achieved the impressive distinction of shooting down four B-17s within eight minutes over Oranienburg between 1430-1438 hrs for his 203rd to 206th victories. Schuck and his group of jets were at 8000 metres when they were directed by the fighter

'Rat catching' – an Me 262 is caught on the gun camera of an American fighter as it is chased to the ground while its pilot attempts to make for the nearest feasible landing place – and that was not always an airfield. The jet fighter was at its most vulnerable shortly after take-off or when coming in to land, when it was moving slowly and it had little room in which to manoeuvre – perfect conditions for an Allied fighter pilot to claim a jet kill

controller towards the bombers, which were reported approaching from the northwest.

To avoid the P-51 escort, Schuck brought his formation into attack on a zig-zag course at 10,000 metres. As the B-17s dropped their bombs on Oranienburg, Schuck fired his four 30 mm MK 108s at a B-17 from a distance of just 300 metres. A wing immediately disintegrated as the German ace turned his attention towards a second *Viermot*. It took hits in its elevator, and the crew baled out of the spiralling aircraft. Soon afterwards, two more bombers exploded after being hit by his cannon fire.

At that moment, Schuck's aircraft was fired at by a P-51 and hit in the left engine. His instruments told him he was at 8200 metres and that power was failing. Mindful of his dwindling fuel supply, Schuck broke away and headed for Jüterbog airfield, although he was uncertain whether the runway there would be intact. With his engine trailing smoke, and chased by a pair of Mustangs, he decided to bale out at a height of 300 metres between Brandenburg-Briest and Jüterbog. He came down safely and was picked up a by a baker on a bicycle. The Knight's Cross holder was taken on the back of the bicycle to the refuge of a nearby mill and offered a cup of coffee. A subsequent German radio message was intercepted, which stated (a little inaccurately);

'Oberleutnant Schuck baled out near Buschkuhnsdorf, near Holzdorf in the Scheinitz district. Successes – 1 Mustang and 2 Boeings. Attacked by 20 Mustangs. Engine caught fire and fuselage shot up. Is with his *Staffel*.'

The Flying Fortresses of the 3rd Air Division targeting Brandenburg-Briest were also intercepted by approximately ten jets from JG 7, but in this case the Americans reported that the attacks were in loose formation, and that the German pilots broke up to make their passes singly and in pairs. Two bombers were lost, with the escort preventing the German score from being higher.

In addition to Schuck's tally, other claims for B-17s were lodged by Oberleutnante Grünberg (two), Stehle and Walter Bohatsch, Oberfähnrich Josef Neuhaus (a former *Zerstörer* pilot), Fähnrich Pfeiffer and Flieger Reiher. In addition to Leutnant Hagenah's Mustang claims, P-51 victories were also credited by Oberleutnant Schall, Leutnant Rademacher and Oberfeldwebels Lennartz and Alfred 'Ali' Griener (who had formerly flown with JG 52 and III./JG 11, and who now had nine kills to his credit). Finally, Feldwebel Pritzl shot down a pair of Thunderbolts.

The claims for nine heavy bombers destroyed by jet fighters tallies with American loss records – a figure which the USAAF reported 'compares favourably for the Germans with their other recent attempts to oppose the Eighth Air Force'.

On the other hand, this was the day dubbed by the Americans as 'the great jet massacre'. Was it? While German documents state five pilots as being killed, at least six from JG 7 are known to have been lost in action or accidents that day. The most senior pilot to die on 10 April was Oberleutnant Franz Schall, commander of 10./JG 7, who perished when his Me 262 rolled into a bomb crater, turned over and exploded following an emergency landing at Parchim. Schall had been awarded the Knight's Cross on 10 October 1944, and on 10 April 1945 had recorded his 133rd victory. A formidable fighter pilot, he had shot down 61 Il-2s over the

Oberleutnant Franz Schall (left), *Staffelkapitän* of 10./JG 7, was killed when his Me 262 rolled into a bomb crater, turned over and exploded after an emergency landing at Parchim following a sortie against the major American raid on 10 April 1945. He is seen here using a field telephone at Achmer while serving with *Kommando Nowotny* in the autumn of 1944

Oberleutnant Hadi Weihs was appointed *Staffelkapitän* of 3./JG 7 upon the death of Oberleutnant Walter Wagner on 10 April 1945

Eastern Front between June 1943 and September 1944 flying with 3./JG 52, and ten P-51s in the defence of the Reich. Schall's place as leader of 10./JG 7 was taken by Oberleutnant Franz Külp.

Also lost on the 10th was Oberleutnant Walter Wagner, who had joined JG 7 from JG 3. His place as commander of 3. *Staffel*, which he had only taken over on 20 March following Waldmann's death, was assumed by Oberleutnant Hadi Weihs. Also killed was Oberleutnant Walter Wever, the son of *General der Flieger* Walther Wever – one of the principal pre-war architects of the Luftwaffe. Wever had flown with distinction over the Eastern Front with 3./JG 51, where, in a period of five minutes, he had shot down three Il-2s on 5 September 1943, and had been awarded the Knight's Cross as recently as 28 January in recognition of his 44 victories. Feldwebel Christoph Schwarz, Unteroffizier Köhler and Gefreiter Heim were also posted as lost in action.

In addition to pilot and ground personnel losses, JG 7 had seen 27 of its precious Me 262s destroyed, with a further eight damaged – a heavy blow from which it would prove very difficult to recover.

Inexorably, the war ground on. Soviet forces had reached the centre of Vienna by 11 April, while that same day American troops arrived at the Elbe, just south of Wittenberge, and only 137 kilometres from the centre of Berlin. OKL signalled *Luftwaffenkommando West* admitting 'available jet and rocket aircraft being neutralised by strong Allied fighter forces, thus impeding landing of our own forces after operations. Alternative landing facilities therefore of decisive importance'.

'Black 4' was one of JG 7's Me 262s flown into Prague-Rusin in mid-April 1945. Note the *Geschwader's* red and blue defence of the Reich fuselage identification band

Another view of Me 262 'Black 4' at Prague-Rusin. It had been fitted with a light blue or grey replacement nose section in the final weeks of the war

At this point, the threat of Allied fighters and the severe damage to the jet bases in northern Germany forced JG 7 to consider an urgent move south to Bavaria. As an interim measure, however, the plan was for the *Geschwaderstab*, together with I./KG(J) 54, to transfer by way of Brandis and Alt Lönnewitz to Saatz and Prague-Rusin, respectively. I. and III./JG 7 were also to be assembled temporarily at Brandis and Alt Lönnewitz, but they never appeared at the former base.

Conditions worked against the transfer from the start. Firstly, the notion that the assigned jet bases in the south were ready was unrealistic. Secondly, the weather was bad, with ten-tenths cloud and rain. Thirdly, Allied fighters were everywhere, making such ferry trips distinctly hazardous – a fact borne out by the recollections of Gefreiter Kurt Lobgesang of 1./JG 7;

'During the afternoon of 14 April 1945, I was attacked by a unit of P-51 Mustangs during a landing flight at Alt Lönnewitz airfield, 15 kilometres east of Torgau/Elbe. I flew Me 262 "White 1". It was the machine of my *Staffelkapitän*, Oberleutnant Hans Grünberg. The Mustang attack came from behind. My Me 262 received hits in the left

engine. Since this began to burn, and I had been wounded, I climbed to 500 metres and baled out, landing by parachute in a pine forest.

'Following attention from doctors at Falkenberg Hospital, I set off at night towards Alt Lönnewitz. There, I met up with some groundcrew from our unit. Early next morning a number of aircraft on the airfield were blown up. A Siebel Si 204 took us with some mechanics to I./JG 7 at Prague-Rusin. Due to my wounds, and fuel shortage, I flew no more operations.'

There is a some debate as to when exactly this event happened. Other sources state that, in fact, it was Oberleutnant Erwin Stahlberg, formerly *Kommandeur* of I./JG 300 and later the *Staffelkapitän* of 9./JG 7, who was shot down on this occasion in the mid-afternoon by a P-51 flown by Capt Clayton K Gross of the 354th FG. Furthermore, there may be an anomaly to Lobgesang's account in as much as that in attempting to land at Alt Lönnewitz on the 11th, Oberleutnant Hans Grünberg was shot down by P-51s – although injured, he baled out safely. His place as *Kapitän* of 1./JG 7 was taken by Oberleutnant Walter Bohatsch on

Oberleutnant Walter Bohatsch was appointed *Staffelkapitän* of 1./JG 7 to replace Oberleutnant Hans Grünberg. Bohatsch made one of the *Geschwader's* final flights when he flew an Me 262 from Saaz, in Soviet-occupied territory, into American captivity

16 April. It is possible either Grünberg had not been flying his usual aircraft on the 11th or Lobgesang was actually flying Bohatsch's jet.

On the 15th, the *Führer's* personal Plenipotentiary for Jet Aircraft, SS-*Obergruppenführer und General der Waffen*-SS Dr. Ing. Kammler took a hand in the fate of JG 7 when he ordered any attempt by the *Geschwader* to move south to cease, instead diverting it to Eger, Saaz and Prague-Rusin, where it was to be placed under the command of Generalmajor Peltz' IX.(J) *Fliegerkorps.*

As it happened, the transfer to these airfields proved challenging. Bad weather cloaked the flight route, but some pilots did make the attempt on 16 April. Several of them were forced to turn back, while most of the rest of the *Geschwader* was scattered across airfields such as Brandenburg-Briest, Kaltenkirchen, Parchim, Saaz, Brandis and Alt Lönnewitz. Eventually, about 25 jets made it to Prague, most of these probably from the 22 Messerschmitts reported on the strength of III./JG 7.

Also on the 15th, a P-51 from the 353rd FG shot down a jet near Riesa, which may have been that piloted by Feldwebel Arno Thimm, formerly of JG 54 but now flying with II./JG 7. He baled out wounded, having possibly become the first operational loss by this *Gruppe.*

February had seen the delivery of ten Me 262A-1as to II./JG 7, while two of the rare Me 262B two-seat trainers had also been delivered to the *Gruppe*, which remained in a state of semi-completion. On 8 April, however, a Major Krächel at Lechfeld signalled *Luftflotte Reich* to advise that 29 pilots of II./JG 7 were ready for operations, presumably having completed training there.

The *Gruppe* personnel then relocated to Brandenburg-Briest, where they were to collect new aircraft from the assembly point there. However, this never happened to any great measure, with the few pilots that received aircraft being ordered to Prague, where they were to be incorporated into those elements of I. and II./JG 7 already there.

British troops stop in their advance across northern Germany to examine an abandoned Me 262A-1a parked in woods off the Hamburg-Leck Autobahn

By the middle of April, fragments of II./JG 7 were at Osterhofen under two Knight's Cross holders, 63-kill ace Major Hermann Staiger, who had previously been *Kommandeur* of I./JG 26 and then II./JG 1, and 71-kill ace Oberleutnant Adolf Glunz, a well-known *Jagdflieger* who had served as *Staffelkapitän* of 6./JG 26. A Battle of Britain ace, Staiger had enhanced his reputation when he shot down three B-17s and claimed two *Herausschüsse* in one mission on 26 April 1944, while Glunz had not been shot down or wounded in 570+ missions.

Despite the odds, JG 7 did not give up. On 17 April, 300 fighters from the Ninth Air Force attacked German airfields at Saatz, Pilsen and Prague-Rusin. At the latter, one Me 262 was destroyed and nine others damaged. Over Saatz, a flight of four jets led by Oberleutnant Hans Grünberg was bounced, and only the leader escaped – it seems the tenacious 'Specker' Grünberg was already back in action, despite having been shot down over Alt Lönnewitz just six days earlier. One of those killed was probably Unteroffizier Fick of 3./JG 7.

About 20 Me 262s from JG 7 managed to fly operations, with Major Späte and Oberleutnante Bohatsch and Stehle each claiming a bomber in the Dresden area. The Eighth Air Force reported three separate attacks by jets, all of which were foiled by the fighter escort. The Americans described the second such attack by some ten Me 262s as 'being driven off by escort fighters. The enemy aircraft came in out of contrails and struck at the bombers from both nose and tail, but were not particularly aggressive and were not successful. One B-17 is known to have been lost as the result of a collision with a jet'.

A B-17 was shot down by Hauptmann Georg-Peter Eder of III./JG 7, now back in action following his injuries sustained in February, near Berlin. However, the unit lost Oberfeldwebel Heinz Arnold of 11./JG 7, who was reported missing in the Thüringer Wald area following a ground-attack mission. Around Prague, Leutnant Fritz Müller and

The jet may well have belonged or been seconded to JG 7's I. *Gruppe*

Oberfeldwebels Pritzl and Anton Schöppler (another former I./JG 5 pilot) all claimed kills.

One of the few pilots from JG 7 operating from Prague in mid-April 1945 was Herbert Schlüter, who had transferred to JG 7 from the luckless *Kommando Stamp*;

'The decision was made to disband *Kommando Stamp* and to incorporate it into JG 7. It was the second half of April, and the situation was hopeless on all fronts. Morale was correspondingly low. Those of us who had come from *Kommando Stamp* became the *Stabsstaffel* of JG 7, and we hardly had contact with the others. I knew no one other than Oberleutnant Stratman, who had been a flying instructor with me. On most days we waited for orders to fly missions. They never came.

'I did fly one mission under the command of Major Späte. We deployed five aircraft against a bomber formation that had attacked Dresden or Leipzig. My aircraft was armed with only two 30 mm cannon and 24 R4M rockets. Shortly before we took off, a man ran over waving frantically and stepped up onto my wing. I opened the canopy and he shouted at me that I had a new version of the R4M rockets, and that I could fire from a distance of 1000 metres.

'Once airborne, we soon had visual contact on the bombers – a formation of B-17s on a northwesterly heading. We climbed above the bombers and attacked from behind at high speed and at a dive angle of 3-5 degrees. When 900 metres from the enemy aircraft, I had two tightly formated bombers in my sight and I pushed the button to fire a salvo of

Seen here on post-war display at the National Air and Space Museum in Washington, DC, Me 262A-1a Wk-Nr. 500491 was formerly 'Yellow 7' of 11./JG 7. This aircraft had once been flown by Oberfeldwebel Heinz Arnold, but on 17 April 1945 it was recorded as unserviceable and he took off in another aircraft to fly a ground-attack mission in the Thüringer Wald area. He never returned. After being made serviceable, 'Yellow 7' was flown from Alt Lönnewitz to Saaz, where it was taken over by Leutnant Fritz Müller. His final flight in the aircraft was on 8 May 1945 when he flew it from Saaz to Lechfeld, surrendering to US forces. The aircraft was assigned the name *"Ginny H."* by its American captors and flown to Cherbourg by 1Lt James K Holt, after whose fiancée the aircraft had been dedicated. It later received the USAAF Foreign Equipment number FE-111 (later T2-111) upon its shipment to the USA

The wingless, shark-like, fuselage of Me 262A-1a Wk-Nr. 112385 'Yellow 8' of 3./JG 7, seen in its entirety on pages 114-115 of this chapter, lies abandoned and forlorn on an airfield near Kassel

rockets. None of them fired! My first thought was perhaps corrosion under the button, and I squeezed the button harder. Again – nothing happened. What I had not fully realised at the time was that my aircraft had sustained several hits from the defensive fire.

'I decided to close in at high speed and pulled the throttle to idle. Unlike piston-engined aircraft, where the propeller acts as a brake and we could adjust our speed to that of the target, the Me 262 flew on without a noticeable reduction in speed. At a distance of about 200 metres, I fired the first burst. The rear of the Boeing – and particularly the stabiliser – was hit badly. Then I fired a burst into the left wing between the No 1 engine and the fuselage. Both engines were hit and the wing between the No 1 engine and the fuselage was ripped open. The wing was on fire, streaking flames. Many parts came away and sailed through the air. I kept firing and flew under the bomber at a distance of 10-20 metres.

'A few seconds later, I felt a shudder in my aircraft as the left wing dipped and at the same time the nose went down. After firing, I had immediately gone back to full power, and now I throttled back to idle and wanted to continue to fly in the horizontal position. I could not move the control column. With all my strength I tried again. Impossible! The control column would not budge. The angle of the wing increased and the air speed reached frightening levels. I had not looked at the air speed indicator even as I had approached the bombers. I knew from past experience that with a dive angle of 5-7 degrees, a speed of 940 km/h could be reached very quickly, and I was flying much faster than that now.

'Many thoughts went through my head. I remembered from conversion training the insistent warnings of the instructors not to reach 1,000 km/h. I had always followed that dictum. I had also thought about the experience of a fellow pilot who had reached, or gone beyond, the 1,000 km/h limit. When he finally regained control he had torn the fuel tank from its fixings and put a huge dent in the bottom of the fuselage.

'Fortunately, at this point the centrifugal forces ceased to be a problem. I was aware of the situation that I found myself in, and that I could not afford to make a mistake. The Me 262 had an electric aileron trim system. Very quickly, I tapped the trim toggle switch and, to my great relief, the left wing lifted a little. I repeated this several times and the wing lifted completely. Now I had to do the same thing to the elevator trim. This also worked. I was flying normally again.

'A little later I set the trim to make the aircraft a little tail-heavy and it shot up rapidly. When the air speed reached 860 km/h, I grabbed the control column and the aircraft was under full control once more. A few minutes later, I spotted a group of P-51 Mustangs – about 50 or 60 of them – 500 metres below me, flying in my direction! I attacked immediately in a 12-15 degree dive. The Americans had obviously seen me, and they discarded their drop tanks and dived away! My air speed increased rapidly, and I had the same problems as before and broke off the attack. I then flew back to Prague-Rusin.

'Take-offs and landings were very difficult there because of the presence of American fighters. That's why I had developed a landing "technique" to

The remains of an Me 262A-1a of JG 7 lie close to the wreck of an Fw 190 at Oberpfaffenhofen. The fuselage carries the shield emblem of JG 7 on both sides of the nose. It appears that an attempt has been made to remove one of the machine's MK 108 cannon

An American serviceman has a snapshot taken as he leans against the fuselage of the Oberpfaffenhofen Me 262 also seen on page opposite. Note the single black chevron visible immediately behind the soldier, indicating that this aircraft may have been the machine of a *Gruppe* Adjutant, and the JG 7 emblem just visible forward of the cockpit

reduce the risk of being shot down. I approached a village with a pointed church spire that lay about 40 kilometres from the airfield. From there, I flew at an altitude of between 30-50 metres with a compass heading to the runway.

'Shortly before I reached the field, I had memorised a spot where I switched the turbines to idle, and as soon as I reached 400 km/h, I activated the landing flap switch. The landing flaps did not activate, however, because of the overload override, and I was able to lower the gear with the emergency switch. The gear came down in seconds using compressed air. The aircraft wanted to rear up, and I had to use the control column to keep it level. I came down with great speed. Now the landing flaps deployed, and behind me I could hear the "barking" of flak. An enemy fighter had evidently tried his luck but had come too late for me.

'After landing, I saw the reasons for my problems. The right wing had some ten to twelve bullet holes in it and the rocket fuel cells had burned, but the projectiles were intact. My aircraft must have been hit before I had tried to fire the R4Ms. The jet engines had not been damaged. Parts of the cowling had been torn off when I had to increase air speed to dive away

American troops gather around the wreck of Me 262A-1a Wk-Nr. 501221 'Yellow 3', believed to have been from 3./JG 7. The jet had been strafing Allied troops near Klötze when it was shot down by ground fire on 21 April 1945. The pilot was captured and the flak battery responsible for its demise awarded a bottle of whisky!

War prize – a GI quickly washes down the tailplane of Wk-Nr. 501221 ready for a snapshot

from the bombers. This would explain the shudder I had felt, and the aerodynamic imbalance had put the Me 262 into the uncontrollable dive to the left. I made my report and mentioned my "probable" kill, since I had no witnesses and could not report what had happened afterwards – but I have no doubt that the badly damaged B-17 could not have remained airborne for long.'

On 19 April, a group of some 20 Me 262s from JG 7 and I./KG(J) 54 operated in scattered elements against bombers in the Dresden-Aussig-Pirna area. The jets claimed five B-17s destroyed – a figure which tallies with American bomber losses. Four of the bombers were victims of one pass by JG 7, when six of its aircraft attacked B-17s of the 3rd Air Division between 1214-1234 hrs when the escort was 'thin' as they made their

bomb run. The fifth Fortress went down to a jet making a pass at '"eight o' clock" against the high squadron of the third group bombing Pirna, the attack being made between the target and the rally point'.

The successful pilots included Hauptmann Späte, Unteroffizier Schöppler and Oberleutnante Bohatsch and Grünberg of I./JG 7, as well as Oberfeldwebel Göbel of III./JG 7.

On 20 April 1945 (Adolf Hitler's 56th birthday), the Allies' mounted a heavy daylight raid by more than 800 US bombers against rail targets in the Berlin area. The RAF would follow that night. The Soviet Army was only some 16 kilometres from the northeastern outskirts of the capital and the city shook with the impact of continuous Russian shelling.

At this point, the command infrastructure of the Luftwaffe jet fighter force in northern Germany fell apart, despite the obsessive efforts of Kammler and Peltz. Conflicting orders were issued regularly by different commands. Those pilots considered good enough from III./KG(J) 6 and I./KG(J) 54 were to be incorporated into III./JG 7. Prague-Rusin signalled *Luftflottenkommando* 6 warning that operations had become impossible due to the presence of Allied fighters over the airfield. Fuel stocks were not neccesarily low, but simply trapped and unable to be moved.

On 25 April, what remnants of I./JG 7 that could be brought together were formed up under the *Kapitän* of 2. *Staffel*, Oberleutnant Fritz Stehle. That same day, JG 7 flew what was probably its last operation against American four-engined bombers,when 276 B-17s of the Eighth Air Force's 1st Air Division attacked the airfield and Skoda factory at Pilsen. Five pilots claimed victories – Major Späte (two), Unteroffizier Schöppler, Oberfeldwebel Göbel, Leutnant Kelb and Unteroffizier Engler, and American losses were indeed six Flying Fortreses. 9./JG 7 pilot Fähnrich Hans-Guido Mütke was forced to land his Me 262 at Zürich-Dubendorf, in Switzerland, due to a lack of fuel.

Evidently photographed some time after the shots featured on the previous page, this view shows that the tail unit of Me 262A-1a Wk-Nr. 501221 'Yellow 3' was unceremoniously sawn off and removed as a trophy by US troops

Above
Me 262A-1a Wk-Nr. 500071 'White 3' of 9./JG 7 gained a certain notoriety when it force-landed at Zürich-Dubendorf, in neutral Switzerland, on 25 April 1945 whilst being flown by Fähnrich Hans-Guido Mütke, who had apparently run low on fuel. Mütke had been flying on a mission to engage US medium bombers over southern Germany. The Swiss authorities recorded that 'The aircraft appears to be in good condition, and gives the impression of not having been in service very long'

Middle
The Swiss wasted little time in moving Hans-Guido Mütke's Me 262 into a hangar, where they conducted a thorough examination of the aircraft

Left
Of particular interest to the Swiss was the new jet engine technology contained within Me 262A-1a Wk-Nr. 500071's Jumo 004s. Here, the aircraft rests on a makeshift cradle and jacks, with the access panels to the port-side engine removed

One of 'White 3's' engines hangs from a mobile crane at Zürich-Dubendorf in readiness for close examination by Swiss aeronautical engineers

After some dispute between the Federal German and Swiss authorities, Me 262A-1a Wk-Nr. 500071 'White 3' was returned to Germany on 30 August 1957, where it was restored and eventually placed on display in the Deutsches Museum in Munich. Here, the dismantled port wing of Wk-Nr. 500071 is lowered into the exhibition hall. Note the R4M rocket rack in the centre of the wing underside

The fighter's fuselage is carefully lowered into the exhibition hall

On the 27th, some of JG 7's Me 262s undertook a ground-attack mission against enemy supply columns near Cottbus, and along with jets from III./KG(J) 6 and I./KG(J) 54, destroyed 65 vehicles. On the way home the fighters ran into some Soviet Il-2s. Despite being low on fuel and ammunition, a few of the Me 262 pilots took on the fearsome Soviet *Shturmoviks*. Herbert Schlüter recalled a mission that he flew around this time;

'I participated in only a handful of missions. I never found out the reason for this. I assume it was the lack of fuel and spare parts as well as the fact that we had more pilots than aircraft. I did, however, fly three missions over the Eastern Front. The orders were to attack Russian troops on the ground. Our aircraft were armed with two MK 108 cannon for this task, and on one occasion a 250-kg bomb was slung under the fuselage. I always flew alone, but did not see much action either because there were no enemy troops in the target area or because I was unable to distinguish between friendly and enemy troops.

'On one of these flights, as I was returning to Prague-Rusin, I encountered an enemy fighter-bomber formation flying on a southwesterly heading at an altitude between 1800-2000 metres. There was a large number of Il-2s in rows of eight to ten, with more flying on a parallel course behind them. Numerous fighters escorted the formation above and below.

'I went for the Il-2s, but the fighters saw me and turned to attack. I could not chance a dogfight. I turned and made off towards the east, only to turn again and renew my attack. Again the fighters spotted me, and I had to break off. It became clear that only the element of surprise would promise success.

Below and bottom right
Me 262A-1a Wk-Nr. 112385, 'Yellow 8' of 3./JG 7 is seen in a hangar at Stendal in mid-April 1945. The aircraft carries the running fox emblem and blue and red fuselage identification band of JG 7. The damage to the fighter's port Jumo unit was caused by 'friendly' airfield defence flak

'After flying to the east once more, I turned and flew at an altitude of 180-200 metres on a southwesterly heading. When I saw the formation above, I pulled up with full power and found a number of fighters in front of me. I was very close when they turned to attack me. Now, with reduced speed, I was able to pull tighter turns.

'A burst of fire and a fighter exploded. I was almost hit by the debris. I was suddenly in the middle of the formation, and since I could not risk a

A rear view of Me 262A-1a Wk-Nr. 112385 'Yellow 8' of 3./JG 7

dogfight, I had to break away again. The Me 262 had lost air speed and accelerated slower than a conventional aircraft, so I decided to play an old trick familiar to fighter pilots of all nations when it was imperative to stick to an opponent who was trying to evade by out-turning his pursuer – deflection shooting. Well I was the pursued, and I had to counter their attempts to hit me. I "dropped" my left wing in order to fake a turn, held the rudder down and flew straight at a declining angle of 12 to 15 degrees at full power as salvos of large calibre, bright red tracer streamed by my left side. The Russians had learned their lessons well. Despite the seriousness of the situation, I could not help but have a little laugh.

'My fuel was too low for another attack. We needed a fuel reserve because of the Mustangs, whose practice it was to wait for us at Prague-Rusin. My "kill" was a probable because I did not have a witness and I did not observe the wreckage hit the ground.'

It is believed that JG 7 accounted for approximately 20 Soviet aircraft destroyed during the last weeks of the war, but in the period 28 April to 1 May, the *Geschwader* lost some ten Me 262s.

On the 28th, Leutnant Fritz Kelb was shot down by flak near Cottbus. He was the only pilot to have scored victories flying both the Me 163 with JG 400 and the Me 262 with JG 7. Leutnant Ernst-Rudolf Geldmacher of 11./JG 7 is believed to have been shot down on take-off from Prague. He was taken to hospital, but later died at the hands of an angry crowd on 15 May 1945.

At sunset on the 29th, I./JG 7 reported 19 aircraft on strength, with 14 serviceable, and 81 pilots with 42 available. Late on the evening of the following day, however, the *Gruppe* reported to XI. *(J) Fliegerkorps*

There is evidence to suggest that Me 262A-1a Wk-Nr. 500443 'Yellow 5', seen here after being captured at Schleswig-Jägel by British forces, may have been the jet of Major Erich Rudorffer, the *Gruppenkommandeur* of I./JG 7. The yellow tactical numeral was adjusted at some time to read '6'. The aircraft was later shipped to England, but in 1946 it voyaged to South Africa, where it was finally scrapped in 1953

that it had 26 aircraft with 13 machines serviceable, and 74 pilots with 64 available.

On 1 May, British forces under Field Marshal Montgomery continued their drive across northern Germany and advanced from the Elbe towards Berlin virtually unopposed. Adolf Hitler had committed suicide in his bunker and there was close-quarter street-fighting with the Russians in the capital. Hermann Göring was under house arrest in southern Germany for attempting to seize control of what remained of the Third Reich as a result of the *Führer's* self-imposed incarceration.

One of the last signals from JG 7 was to report the ground elements of the *Geschwaderstab* at Mühldorf. A week later, on 7 May, II./JG 7 was reported by *Luftflotte Reich* to be at Gettorf 'minus aircraft'.

An Arado Ar 234 reconnaissance jet, formerly of 1.(F)/33 and captured in Denmark, was shipped to England and included in the exhibition of Axis aircraft held at the Royal Aircraft Establishment (RAE) Farnborough. It is seen here at Farnborough with Me 262A-1a Wk-Nr. 111690 'White 5', which had been flown to Fassberg by Oberleutnant Fritz Stehle, *Staffelkapitän* of 2./JG 7, on 8 May 1945. This Me 262 was known to have been equipped with an EZ 42 gyroscopic gunsight, and would have been the machine in which Stehle shot down a Russian Yak-9 over Czechoslovakia, though some sources state that it was in fact a Soviet P-39 flown by Lt S G Stepanov of 129 GIAP (22 GIAD). The British assigned the aircraft the Air Ministry number '80', and it was subsequently test flown in the UK, before being shipped to Canada in August 1946, where it was apparently burned during fire-fighting exercises on an RCAF base in Ontario. Some sources maintain that the remains were later buried on a farm!

A rear view of Me 262A-1a Wk-Nr. 111690 'White 5', formerly flown by Oberleutnant Fritz Stehle, *Staffelkapitän* of 2./JG 7 in 1945, but seen here outside the hangars at the RAE Farnborough wearing an RAF roundel

Me 262A-1a Wk-Nr. 500210 'Yellow 17' was surrendered by Leutnant Hans Dorn of 3./JG 7 at Fassberg on 8 May 1945. On 27 May it was flown by British pilot Clive Gosling to Schleswig, via Lübeck. Assigned the British number 'Air Min 52' and given the RAF serial VH509, it was subsequently flown to Farnborough, via Melsbroek and Manston, on 9 June 1945. It was then placed in storage at No 6 Maintenance Unit at Brize Norton on 29 June, before being shipped to Canada on 23 August 1946. Allegedly, it ended up on an airfield near Toronto, where it was eventually scrapped

In what is believed to have been the last jet sortie of the war, the acting commander of I./JG 7, Oberleutnant Fritz Stehle, shot down a Yak-9 over Czechoslovakia on 8 May whilst flying one of the last airworthy aircraft of the composite battle command *Gefechtsverband Hogeback*. Stehle then made his way to Fassberg to surrender.

Also on the morning of the 8th, the few operational Me 262s of I./JG 7 flew ground-attack missions over the Cottbus-Berlin *Autobahn*. Oberleutnant Walter Bohatsch recalled;

'The Me 262 was not very suitable for this task due to its high speed. After landing back at base (Saaz), my aircraft was taken out of service due to excessively high engine temperatures.

'There were no longer any ground personnel on the airfield as they had all begun to make their way West. Amongst the remaining pilots was Oberleutnant Stehle, who commented, "The war is over, and any pilots

Me 262A-1a Wk-Nr. 500210 'Yellow 17' of 3./JG 7 (left) is seen here at Fassberg with Me 262A-1a Wk-Nr. 110800, which was originally piloted by Unteroffizier Günther Engler also of 3./JG 7

wishing to fly anywhere specific can carry on". Someone suggested we fly to Fassberg. However, as my machine was unserviceable I would have to find a substitute aircraft. My old "grinder" was out of action, so I decided to take "White 4", and tested the engines by running them at high speed, which showed that everything appeared to be in order. Unfortunately, the fuel tank was only half full, and as my desire was to fly east to Linz-Horsching, my fuel would be barely adequate. I then heard the "Free Austria" radio announce that the Russian spearhead armour had reached Linz, so trying to reach Horsching was no longer an option.

Above and below
Flying into Fassberg from Saaz, in Czechoslovakia, on 8 May to surrender to British forces was Me 262A-1a Wk-Nr. 110007 'Yellow 5', piloted by Unteroffizier Anton Schöppler of 3./JG 7. It may have been assigned the Air Ministry number '79', and it is believed to have been scrapped immediately post-war at Fassberg

Me 262A-1a Wk-Nr. 500226
was briefly operated by the
*Industrieschutzschwarm
Memmingen* (Memmingen test
facility defence flight), before being
transferred to JG 7 in February 1945.
After a further period at Munich-
Riem, it was then flown by
Oberleutnant Walter Bohatsch,
Staffelkapitän of 1./JG 7, as 'White 4'
from Saaz, in Czechoslovakia, to the
small military airfield at Dedelstorf,
67 km north of Braunschweig, on 8
May 1945, where it was surrendered
to US forces. Visible here is the
warning applied by the Americans
to the jet fighter's tail section for
any aspiring souvenir hunters to
KEEP OFF

The starboard side of Me 262A-1a,
Wk-Nr. 500226 'White 4' of 1./JG 7
was adorned with a further, crude
warning – *GUNS LOADED*

'Oberleutnant Grünberg, with whom I had flown for two years, firstly in
JG 3 and then with JG 7, proposed that I fly with him to Kaltenkirchen,
which was near his home. However, as I knew I did not have enough fuel to
reach Kaltenkirchen, I decided to make my way in the direction of Fassberg.
The take-off was trouble free, but I noticed that neither the compass nor the
radio were working.

'The weather was good, and as it was around 1700 hrs, I decided to fly
into the sun in a westerly direction. Below me, all the Russian-occupied airfields gave me a green light to land, which I simply ignored. After a while I
knew that I must have left the Russian occupied area, but I also knew that
I would not reach Fassberg, as my fuel was evaporating quickly.

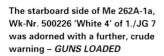

Me 262A-1a Wk-Nr. 112372 'Red 2' was delivered to JG 7 in late March 1945. It was later captured by the British at Schleswig and assigned the number '51' by the Air Ministry. On 1 June the fighter was flown to Twente, in Holland, by Flt Lt Arend, where it is believed to have received some repair work, before flying on to Farnborough. It was test flown by the British until November 1945, and is the only surviving Me 262 in the UK

'I now knew that I was in the American occupied area, and I spotted an airfield below, recognisable by the black and white roofed buildings around the perimeter, but no aircraft were in sight.

'I decided to land, and during my approach the port engine suddenly stopped due to lack of fuel. I managed to land on one engine, and as I rolled to a stop, there were two American Jeeps waiting to greet me, and make me a prisoner of war. However I had no idea as to where I had landed.

'As far as I know, it is probable that Oberleutnant Hans Grünberg and I flew the two very last Luftwaffe-piloted Me 262s of the war from Saaz airfield on 8 May 1945.'

Adorned with British roundels, JG 7's Wk-Nr. 112372 'Red 2' undergoes engine testing at either Farnborough or Brize Norton

APPENDICES

APPENDIX 1

KNIGHT'S CROSS HOLDERS OF *JAGDGESCHWADER* 7

Name	Date of Award	Victories	To JG 7 from
Oberfeldwebel Hermann Buchner	KC 20/7/44	58	II./SG 2
Hauptmann Georg-Peter Eder	Oak 25/11/44	78	*Kdo. Nowotny*
Major Heinrich Ehrler	Oak 2/8/43	208	*Kommodore* JG 5
Oberleutnant Adolf Glunz	Oak 24/6/44	71	II./JG 26
Major Ludwig Grözinger	KC 15/11/42	(BP)	IV./KG 53
Oberleutnant Hans Grünberg	KC 8/7/44	82	5./JG 3
Hauptmann Heinz Gutmann	KC 4/4/44	(BP)	I./KG 53
Major Erich Hohagen	KC 5/10/41	55	III./EJG 2
Leutnant Viktor Petermann	KC 29/2/44	64	II./JG 52
Leutnant Rudolf Rademacher	KC 30/9/44	126	EJG 1
Major Erich Rudorffer	Swo 25/1/45	222	II./JG 54
Oberleutnant Franz Schall	KC 10/10/44	133	*Kdo. Nowotny*
Oberleutnant Walter Schuck	Oak 30/9/44	206	10./JG 5
Major Wolfgang Späte	Oak 23/4/42	99	*Kommodore* JG 400
Major Hermann Staiger	KC 16/7/41	63	II./JG 1
Major Gerhard Stamp	KC 24/3/42	(BP) 4	*Kdo. Stamp*
Oberst Johannes Steinhoff	Swo 28/7/44	176	*Kommodore* JG 77
Oberleutnant Hans Waldmann	Oak 1/3/45	134	III./JG 3
Major Theodor Weissenberger	Oak 2/8/43	208	I./JG 5
Oberleutnant Walter Wever	KC 28/1/45	44	I./JG 51

Key
(BP) – Bomber Pilot
KC – Knight's Cross
Oak – Oakleaves to Knight's Cross
Swo – Swords to Knight's Cross

COLOUR PLATES

1

Me 262A-1a 'White 7' of Oberfeldwebel Hermann Buchner, *Kommando Nowotny*, Lechfeld, October 1944

'White 7' is finished in the typical colours of *Kommando Nowotny*. Virtually all of the unit's jets carried their tactical numbers in white, forward of the cockpit, and had a yellow band applied to the fuselage forward of the Balkenkreuz. The fuselage itself is finished in two shades of green, possibly RLM 82 and RLM 83. A number of *Kdo. Nowotny's* Me 262s boasted the so-called 'tadpole' marked tailplanes as they had been delivered to the final assembly plant as pre-built units, but it would appear that this aircraft did not, retaining a more common late-war mottling.

2

Me 262A-1a 'Green 1' of Major Rudolf Sinner, *Stab* III./JG 7, Brandenburg-Briest, January 1945

It seems that Rudolf Sinner was assigned two jets, although it is unlikely that they were both at Brandenburg-Briest at the same time. This Me 262 is finished in an unusual diagonally striped pattern of RLM 82 and RLM 83 bands running, from the port side, right to left along the fuselage. The aircraft's tactical number '3' is in green immediately below the *Geschwader* emblem on the nose. Forward of the Balkenkreuz is the double chevron marking denoting a *Gruppenkommandeur's* aircraft, and aft of it is the blue and red defence of the Reich identification band superimposed with the vertical bar of III. *Gruppe*. It is likely that the Hakenkreuz was applied in solid white.

3

Me 262A-1a 'Green 1' of Major Rudolf Sinner, *Stab* III./JG 7, Brandenburg-Briest, January 1945

Sinner's 'second', or 'other', Me 262 as *Kommandeur* of III./JG 7 features a pattern in reverse to that of the preceding aircraft. This machine is finished in diagonally striped pattern of RLM 82 and RLM 83 bands running, from the port side, left to right along the fuselage. The individual markings appear to be identical, with the aircraft's tactical number '3' in green immediately below the *Geschwader* emblem, the double chevron marking of a *Gruppenkommandeur's* aircraft, the blue and red defence of the Reich identification band superimposed with the vertical bar of III. *Gruppe* and with a Hakenkreuz in solid white.

4

Me 262A-1a Wk-Nr. 111588 'White 5' of 11./JG 7, Brandenburg-Briest, January 1945

This Leipheim-built III. *Gruppe* Me 262 wears a standard late-war Luftwaffe finish – probably a mottle of RLM 81 and RLM 83 applied over a base of RLM 76. The aircraft's tactical number is in white, but it does not carry the *Geschwader* emblem of JG 7. The Werknummer has been stencilled in a standard location on the tailplane beneath the Hakenkreuz but there are some unusual markings on the tail assembly and rudder – a vertical chevron and the number '17'. These may have been factory-applied part references.

5

Me 262A-1a Wk-Nr. 110800 'White 7' of Unteroffizier Günther Engler, 3./JG 7, February 1945

This aircraft appears to have been finished in a heavy 'stipple' effect – probably random, rough patches of RLM 81 and RLM 83 over a base colour of RLM 76. The aircraft carries the running fox emblem of JG 7 in the commonly seen location on the nose and the Hakenkreuz on the tail is in solid white – a common feature on many of JG 7's aircraft. It would seem that the aircraft also had the blue and red defence of the Reich identification band. The tops of the engine nacelles are finished in more of a single colour, probably RLM 83.

6

Me 262A-1a 'Green 4' of Major Theodor Weissenberger, *Geschwaderstab* JG 7, Brandenburg-Briest, February-March 1945

Some sources state that the *Geschwader* shield applied to Major Weissenberger's aircraft was backed in white, but this seems unlikely, and indeed, careful study of the photograph of this aircraft would suggest it was finished in the usual light blue. However, what does seem to be the case is that the upper third of light blue on the emblem is unusually large in proportion, or that the whole emblem has been partially applied over another. The tactical number '4' in green is directly below the emblem. The aircraft was probably finished in an overall coat of RLM 83, with RLM 76 or RLM 77 undersurfaces, breaking up to some degree on the tail assembly. The aircraft carries extended horizontal bars in black, outlined in white, denoting the *Kommodore's* aircraft, as well as JG 7's distinctive blue and red defence of the Reich identification band.

7

Me 262A-1a 'Green 3' of *Geschwaderstab* JG 7, Brandenburg-Briest, February-March 1945

This aircraft is finished in a most distinctive camouflage of crude, essentially horizontal lines in RLM 82, most evident over the nose section, while the area below the cockpit features a darker single tone, breaking up again towards the rear of the fuselage and over the tail assembly. The aircraft is fitted with 21 cm WGr 21 mortar tubes, and the tip of its nose is finished in solid RLM 82. The tactical number '3' is in green below the running fox shield of JG 7 and the single chevron in black, outlined in white, denoting the aircraft of an adjutant, is forward of the Balkenkreuz, aft of which is the *Geschwader's* blue and red defence of the Reich identification band. Note what would appear to be the very worn condition of the paintwork on the forward section of the engine nacelle.

8

Me 262A-1a 'White 7' of III./JG 7, Brandenburg-Briest, April 1945

This R4M-equipped Messerschmitt has a very standard finish of RLM 83 over RLM 76. The tactical number '7' is in white, the vertical bar of III. *Gruppe*, also in white, has been painted onto the unit's blue and red defence of the Reich identification bands, each band measuring 450 mm in width to conform to OKL requirements. The *Geschwader* emblem has been applied in its usual location.

9

Me 262A-1a 'Green 3' of *Geschwaderstab* JG 7, Brandenburg-Briest, April 1945

'Green 3' features a very heavy and somewhat shiny application of dark green, probably RLM 83, over most of its airframe, although patches of the lighter RLM 82 are evident on the uppersurface of the nose and breaking down into the side of the nose section. The tactical number '3' is quite unusual in style, and there appear to be no other markings, nor a defence of the Reich fuselage band. The Hakenkreuz on the tail is in solid white, and it would appear that the rudder is lighter in colour (rather than being attributable to light), suggesting a replacement part.

10

Me 262A-1a 'Green 2' of *Geschwaderstab* JG 7, Brandenburg-Briest, April 1945

True to JG 7's tendency to experiment with camouflage schemes, this Me 262 is finished in a very non-standard 'tortoise shell' effect. It is possible that this was applied in RLM 82 over a base of RLM 76. The tactical number, below the running fox *Geschwader* shield, was probably in green, while the defence of the Reich fuselage band appears to be absent. The aircraft carried a single chevron and extended horizontal bars on either side of the Balkenkreuz, possibly denoting its assignment to the *Geschwader* Operations Officer, or perhaps it was yet another machine flown by the *Kommodore*, Major Weissenberger. The Hakenkreuz was probably finished in solid white.

11

Me 262A-1a Wk-Nr. 112385 'Yellow 8' of 3./JG 7, Stendal, April 1945

This well-known machine, which was found in a hangar at Stendal by advancing Allied forces in mid April 1945, was finished in patches of RLM 81 over a base coat of RLM 82, with undersides in RLM 76. All other markings – unit emblem, tactical number, defence of the Reich fuselage band and Werknummer – are standard style in the usual locations.

12

Me 262A-1a Wk-Nr. 501221 'Yellow 3' of 3./JG 7, Klötze, April 1945

A typically finished late-war aircraft produced under the supervision of Messerschmitt Regensburg, 'Yellow 3' nevertheless has two distinguishing features. Firstly, the numerals of the stencilled Werknummer, in black, appear closer together and in a slightly more forward position beneath the Hakenkreuz than was usually the case. And secondly, its blue and red defence of the Reich fuselage band is marked with the vertical bar of III. *Gruppe*, despite the jet being shot down by Allied troops over Klötze on 21 April 1945 while actually being flown by a 3. *Staffel* pilot.

13

Me 262A-1a 'Red 3' possibly from I./JG 7, northern Germany, April-May 1945

It is possible that this aircraft belonged to I./JG 7. The fighter features a large tactical number in red outlined in white applied to the rear nose area, and would appear to have been finished in a blend of RLM 81 and RLM 83, with RLM 76 undersurfaces. It is unlikely the aircraft carried any other recognition features other than a standard late war fuselage Balkenkreuz and Hakenkreuz.

14

Me 262A-1a Wk-Nr. 111918 of *Gruppenstab* I./JG 7, western Germany, April-May 1945

This Leipheim-built machine featured an application of RLM 83 along the top of the fuselage, leaving an unusually high demarcation line at which point the colour broke down into a mottle of RLM 83 and 82 over RLM 76. The aircraft also boasts the running fox emblem of JG 7, a single black chevron outlined in white forward of the Balkenkreuz that indicates its assignment to a *Gruppen* Adjutant, and a standard blue and red defence of the Reich fuselage band. The Werknummer has been applied by stencil in black beneath a black Hakenkreuz outlined in white, which would appear to have been partially oversprayed.

15

Me 262A-1a Wk-Nr. 500443 'Yellow 6' of I./JG 7, Schleswig-Jägel, May 1945

Built by Messerschmitt Regensburg, this Me 262 was captured at Schleswig-Jägel by British forces and may originally have been the aircraft of Major Erich Rudorffer, the *Gruppenkommandeur* of I./JG 7. The yellow tactical numeral was adjusted at some stage to a smaller than usual '6'. The German Balkenkreuz has been overpainted by a bold British roundel, and the Hakenkreuz replaced by British rudder bars, although the Werknummer remains. The aircraft is devoid of any other markings, and appears to have been finished in a wash of RLM 82, under which panel lines are clearly visible.

16

Me 262A-1a Wk-Nr. 500071 'White 3' of Fähnrich Hans-Guido Mütke, 9./JG 7, Brandenburg-Briest, April 1945

The much-photographed aircraft of Fähnrich Hans-Guido Mütke of 9./JG 7 was finished in a generally standard late-war scheme of RLM 82 and RLM 83, with mottling in the same colours under a demarcation line at about the midway point running along the length of the fuselage. Of interest is the Swiss report compiled after Mütke's landing at Zurich, which read 'Paintwork: Matt finish thinly applied paint. Uppersurfaces moss green with olive green patches/light blue underneath. Codes: Both sides of the fuselage: 3+I painted in white. On the rear fuselage are painted a blue and red band 0.9 m wide. On the fin the number 500071 with a Swastika on both sides in black. On the wing uppersurface a small + in white and on the underside a black +'.

17

Me 262A-1a of JG 7, Oberpfaffenhofen, May 1945

This aircraft, bearing the single black chevron of a *Gruppe* Adjutant, was photographed on a scrap heap at the end of the war. A splinter pattern of RLM 81 and RLM 82 appears to have been applied to the upper fuselage surface, but breaks up at a quite high demarcation point along the fuselages sides, with random patches of both RLM 81 and RLM 82 over RLM 76 from that point. Of note on this aircraft is a variation of the *Geschwader* emblem, which appears to feature the running fox with its legs crossed, as opposed to the standard marking where the legs were open in stride.

18

Me 262A-1a 'Black 4' of JG 7, Prague-Rusin, May 1945

The most distinguishing feature of 'Black 4' was its replacement nose section, which had been left in a light blue or grey primer. Its tactical number, which was outlined in white, was of the 'closed' variety, and it had the blue and red defence of the Reich fuselage band of JG 7 aft of the Balkenkreuz. Unless the *Geschwader* emblem had been applied to the original nose section, it would appear that no such marking was ever carried by this jet in the standard location.

19

Me 262A-1a Wk-Nr. 500226 'White 4' of Oberleutnant Walter Bohatsch, 1./JG 7, Dedelstorf, May 1945

This jet was briefly flown by the *Industrieschutzschwarm Memmingen* (Memmingen test facility defence flight), prior to being transferred to JG 7 in February 1945. After a further period at Munich-Riem, it was then flown by Oberleutnant Walter Bohatsch, *Staffelkapitän* of 1./JG 7, as 'White 4' from Saaz, in Czechoslovakia, to the small military airfield at Dedelstorf, 67 km north of Braunschweig, on 8 May 1945, where it was surrendered to US forces. It was finished in standard RLM 82/83 colours, devoid of any unit emblem, but with JG 7's blue and red defence of the Reich fuselage band. The tactical '4', in white, was of the 'open' variety, the Hakenkreuz in solid black with no outline, and the aircraft had at some point received a replacement rudder that was left in bare grey wooden primer. The words *KEEP OFF* were crudely applied by the jet's American captors on its nose section and lower tail assembly.

20

Me 262A-1a Wk-Nr. 500210, 'Yellow 17' of Leutnant Hans Dorn, 3./JG 7, Fassberg, May 1945

Representative of a number of JG 7's aircraft in the final weeks of the war, Hans Dorn's 'Yellow 17' bore some similarity to Bohatsch's aircraft. Finished in RLM 82 and RLM 83, the only unit marking was the blue and red defence of the Reich fuselage band.

21

Me 262A-1a Wk-Nr. 110007 'Yellow 5' of Unteroffizier Anton Schöppler, 3./JG 7, Fassberg, May 1945

Leipheim-built 'Yellow 5' carried the vertical black bar of III. *Gruppe*, yet Anton Schöppler is believed to have flown with 3. *Staffel* of I./JG 7. This may have been an available III. *Gruppe* machine acquired by Schöppler in the last, chaotic days of the war. Finished in a standard RLM 82/83 mottle pattern with RLM 76 undersides, the aircraft featured the running fox shield of JG 7, the blue and red defence of the Reich fuselage band and a Werknummer stencilled in black beneath a black Hakenkreuz outlined in white. The upper panels of the port-side Jumo unit have been replaced as far back as the wing leading edge, probably due to battle damage.

22

Me 262A-1a Wk-Nr. 111690 'White 5' of Oberleutnant Fritz Stehle, 2./JG 7, Fassberg, May 1945

Fritz Stehle's machine was finished in overall RLM 82, with evidence of panel lines beneath the paint. The British had applied a roundel over the Balkenkreuz, and the tail Hakenkreuz had been painted out. Bare metal replacement Jumo engine panels had also been fitted by its captors at some stage.

23

Me 262A-1a Wk-Nr. 500491 '888' *"Ginny H."* of 'Watson's Whizzers', Lechfeld, June 1945

Regensburg-built Wk-Nr. 500491 was originally 'Yellow 7' of 11./JG 7's Oberfeldwebel Heinz Arnold and Leutnant Fritz Müller. It is depicted here in the markings of 'Watson's Whizzers', who would ferry the aircraft from Lechfeld to Cherbourg. The original German RLM 82-based finish has been left untouched, but the Balkenkreuz has been overpainted with a USAAF marking and the Hakenkreuz has been oversprayed – although this may have been an original feature. Nose art depicting the jet-powered Donald Duck emblem of the 'Whizzers' has been applied to the forward nose section. The tip of the nose is in red and the 'Whizzers'' code number 888 has been applied by stencil beneath the horizontal stabiliser. The aircraft was assigned the name *"Ginny H."* by its American captors and flown to Cherbourg by 1Lt James K Holt, after whose fiancée the aircraft had been dedicated. The fighter subsequently received the USAAF Foreign Equipment number FE-111 (later T2-111) upon its shipment to the USA, and it was eventually put on display at the National Air and Space Museum in Washington, DC.

24

Me 262A-1a Wk-Nr. 112372 'Red 2' of JG 7, Schleswig, May 1945

This aircraft was passed onto JG 7 by III./EJG 2. It has been suggested that the red '2' on a blue shield may have been an emblem adopted by the latter unit, but equally it could have been a late variation of a JG 7 tactical number with a link to the *Geschwader's* light blue shield. Certainly, the aircraft carried the blue and red defence of the Reich fuselage band of JG 7 and was finished in an overall application of RLM 82. After its acquisition by the British, RAF fuselage roundels and tail markings were applied. Photographs suggest an area of the fuselage forward of the starboard-side Balkenkreuz was replaced, probably due to combat damage.

BIBLIOGRAPHY

UNPUBLISHED SOURCES

Interview transcript, Walter Hagenah, June 1976 (via Boyne)

Interview transcript, Karl Schnörrer, October 1978 (via Boyne)

Interview transcript, Walter Windisch, 1976 (via Boyne)

'My time with the Me 262', private recollections by Herbert Schlüter

Correspondence with Hermann Buchner and Herbert Schlüter

Flugbuch, Oberleutnant Hans Peter Waldmann & Fähnrich Feldwebel Heinrich Janssen

JG 7 Development Chart prepared by Manfred Griehl (author collection)

UK NATIONAL ARCHIVES:

AIR20/7708 – The Western Front 1-14 February 1945 and 15-28 February 1945: Daily Situation Reports issued by OKL Operations Staff Ia

AIR22/418 – Eighth and Fifteenth USAAF weekly Intelligence summaries: Nos. 52-82 1944 Nov - 1945 June

AIR40/1460 – Intelligence Reports 'M' series Nos 1-50 (incomplete): GAF

AIR40/2021 –- Combined Operational Planning Committee: sixteenth periodic report on enemy daylight fighter defences and interception tactics 1-30 April 1945

DEFE/3 505, 562, 566, 568 – Admiralty: Operational Intelligence Centre: Intelligence from Intercepted German, Italian and Japanese Radio Communications, 1945 Feb 6-10

HW5/626, 686, 692 and 698 – Government Code and Cypher School: German Section: Reports of German Army and Air Force High Grade Machine Decrypts (CX/FJ, CX/JQ and CX/MSS Reports)

Das Oberkommando der Luftwaffe Kriegstagebuch 1 February - 7 April 1945 (NAARS/Microfilm T-321/Roll 10) (via Irving)

'Zugang aus Industrie' Stand 31/3/45 and 10/4/45 (prepared for OKL Führungsstab)

PUBLISHED REFERENCES

Jägerblatt Nr. 3/XLIII, July/August 1994

Jägerblatt Nr. 4/1996

Luftwaffe im Focus Spezial No. 2 – 1945: Die letzten Monate der Luftwaffe, Luftfahrtverlag Start, 2006

BALOUS, MIROSLAV & RAJLICH, Jiri Messerschmitt Me 262, JaPo, Hradec Kralove

BOEHME, MANFRED, JG 7 The World's First Jet Fighter Unit 1944/1945, Schiffer, Atglen, PA, 1992

BUCHNER, HERMANN, Stormbird Flying through fire as a Luftwaffe ground attack pilot and Me 262 ace, Hikoki Publications, Aldershot, 2000

FOREMAN, JOHN & HARVEY, The Messerschmitt Me 262 Combat Diary, Air Research Publications, Walton-on-Thames, 1990

FORSYTH, ROBERT, JV 44 – The Galland Circus, Classic Publications, Burgess Hill, 1996

FREEMAN, ROGER A, Mighty Eighth War Diary, Jane's, London, 1981

GIRBIG, WERNER, Jagdgeschwader 5 'Eismeerjäger' – Eine Chronik aus Dokumenten und Berichten 1941-1945, Motorbuch Verlag, Stuttgart, 1976

GREEN, BRETT AND EVANS, BENJAMIN, Stormbird Colors: Construction, Camouflage and Markings of the Me 262, Eagle Editions, Hamilton, 2002

HAMMEL, ERIC, Air War Europe – America's Air War against Germany in Europe and North Africa: Chronology 1942-1945, Pacifica Press, 1994

HESS, WILLIAM N, German Jets versus the US Army Air Force, Specialty Press, North Branch, 1996

LORANT, JEAN-YVES & GOYAT, RICHARD, Jagdgeschwader 300 "Wilde Sau" Volume Two September 1944 - May 1945, Eagle Editions, Hamilton, 2007

MOMBEEK, ERIC, Eismeerjäger. Zur Geschichte des Jagdgeschwaders 5 Band 1 Zerstörerstaffel und Jabostaffel, ASBL La Porte d'Hoves, undated

MORGAN, HUGH, Me 262 Stormbird Rising, Osprey, London, 1994

MORGAN, HUGH & WEAL, JOHN, Osprey Aircraft of the Aces 17 - German Jet Aces of World War 2, Osprey, London, 1998

O'CONNELL, DAN, Messerschmitt Me 262: The Production Log 1941-1945, Classic Publications, 2005

OBERMAIER, ERNST, Die Ritterkreuzträger der Luftwaffe 1939-1945 – Band I Jagdflieger, Verlag Dieter Hoffmann, Mainz, 1966 & 1982

PRIEN, JOCHEN & STEMMER, Gerhard, *Messerschmitt Bf 109 im Einsatz bei der II./Jadgeschwader 3*, Struve-Druck, Eutin, undated

PRIEN, JOCHEN, RODEIKE, PETER & STEMMER, GERHARD, *Messerschmitt Bf 109 im Einsatz bei Stab und I./Jagdgeschwader 27*, Struve-Druck, Eutin, undated

PRIEN, JOCHEN, RODEIKE, PETER & STEMMER, GERHARD, *Messerschmitt Bf 109 im Einsatz bei der II./Jagdgeschwader 27*, Struve-Druck, Eutin, undated

PRIEN, JOCHEN, RODEIKE, PETER & STEMMER, GERHARD, *Messerschmitt Bf 109 im Einsatz bei III. und IV./Jagdgeschwader 27*, Struve-Druck, Eutin, undated

PRIEN, JOCHEN, *Geschichte des Jagdgeschwaders 77 Teil 4 1944-1945*, Struve-Druck, Eutin, undated

RAJLICH, JIRI, KOKOSKA, STANISLAV & JANDA, ALES, *Luftwaffe over Czech Territory 1945*, JaPo, Hradec Kralove

RUST, KENN C, *Fifteenth Air Force Story*, Historical Aviation Album, Temple City, CA, 1976

RUST, KENN C & HESS, WILLIAM N, *The German Jets and the US Army Air Force*, A.A.H.S. Journal, Fall 1963

SHORES, CHRISTOPHER, *Luftwaffe Fighter Units Europe 1942-45*, Osprey Publishing, London, 1979

SCHUCK, WALTER, *Abschuss! Von der Me 109 zur Me 262: Erinnerungen an die Luftkämpfe beim Jagdgeschwader 5 und 7*, Helios Verlag, Aachen, 2007

SMITH, J RICHARD & CREEK, EDDIE J, Me 262 *Volume One*, Classic Publications, Burgess Hill, 1997

SMITH, J RICHARD & CREEK, EDDIE J, Me 262 *Volume Two*, Classic Publications, Burgess Hill, 1998

SMITH, J RICHARD & CREEK, EDDIE J, Me 262 *Volume Three*, Classic Publications, Crowborough, 2000

SMITH, J RICHARD & CREEK, EDDIE J, Me 262 *Volume Four*, Classic Publications, Crowborough, 2000

STEINHOFF, JOHANNES, *The Last Chance – The Pilot's Plot Against Göring*, Hutchinson, London, 1977

WEAL, JOHN, *Osprey Aviation Elite Units 6 - Jagdgeschwader 54 'Grünherz'*, Osprey Publishing, Oxford, 2001

WEAL, JOHN, *Osprey Aircraft of the Aces 25 - Messerschmitt Bf 110 Zerstörer Aces of World War 2*, Osprey Publishing, Oxford, 1999

USEFUL WEBSITES

Aces of the Luftwaffe @ www.luftwaffe.cz

The Luftwaffe 1933-1945 @ www.ww2.dk

INDEX

References to illustrations are shown in **bold**. Plates are shown with page and caption locators in brackets.